As Long As He Needs Me

from the Broadway musical *OLIVER!*

Words and Music by Lionel Bart

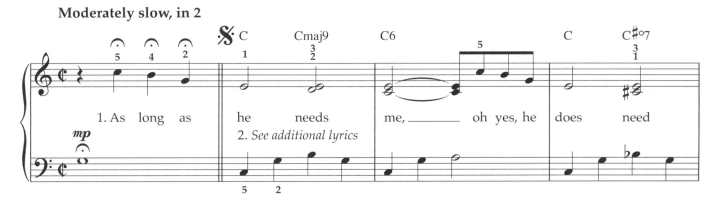

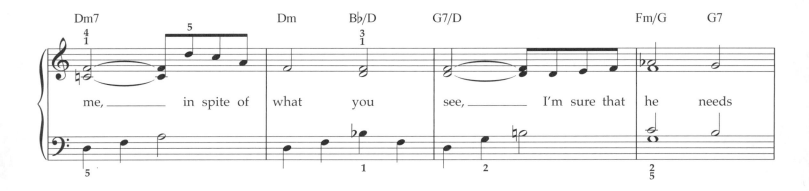

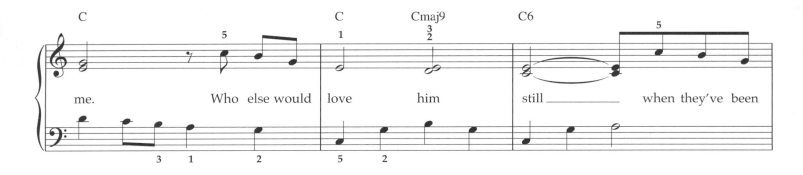

he needs me. I miss him so much___ when he is

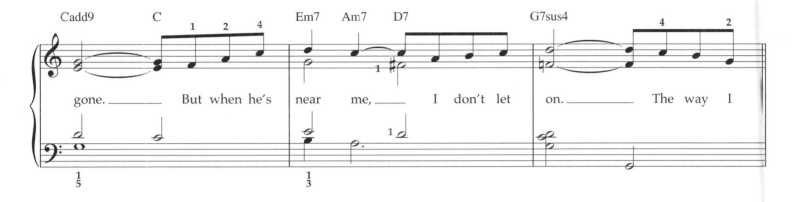

gone.___ But when he's near me,___ I don't let on.___ The way I

feel in - side,___ the love I have to

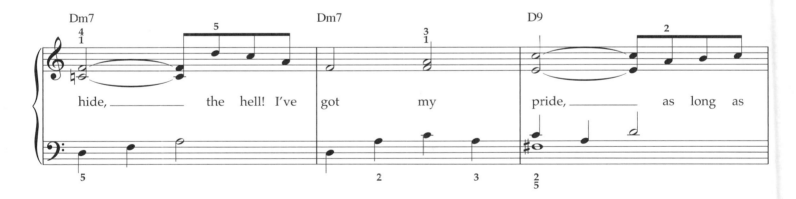

hide,___ the hell! I've got my pride,___ as long as

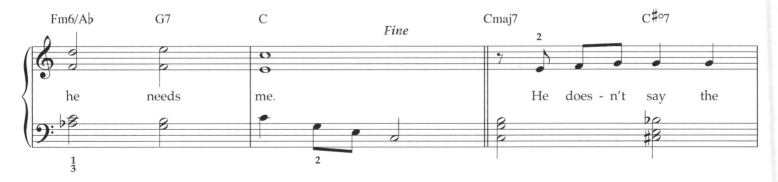

he needs me. He does - n't say the

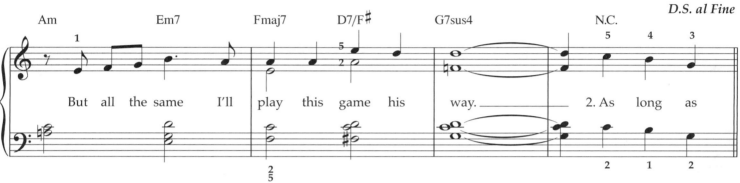

D.S. al Fine

Additional lyrics

2. As long as he needs me,
   I know where I must be,
   I'll cling on steadfastly
   As long as he needs me.

   As long as life is long,
   I'll love him right or wrong,
   And somehow I'll be strong
   As long as he needs me.

   If you are lonely,
   Then you will know
   When someone needs you,
   You love them so.

   I won't betray his trust,
   Though people say I must,
   I've got to stay true, just
   As long as he needs me.

Any Dream Will Do

from *JOSEPH AND THE AMAZING TECHNICOLOR® DREAMCOAT*

Music by Andrew Lloyd Webber
Lyrics by Tim Rice

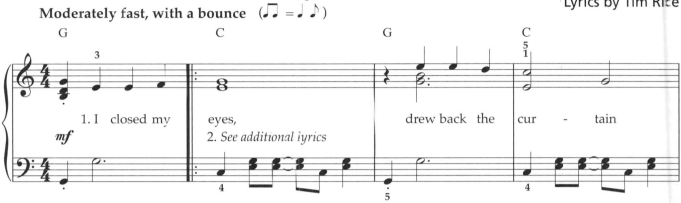

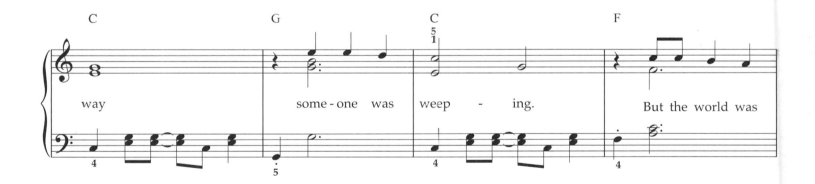

8

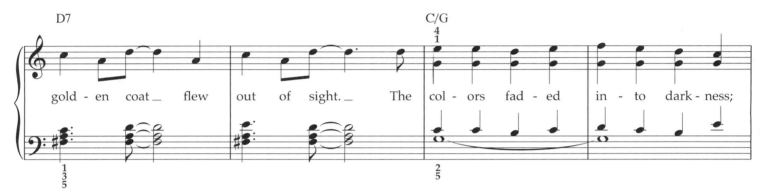

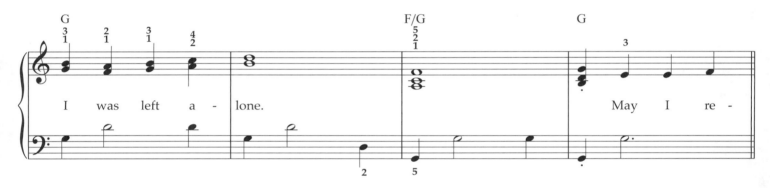

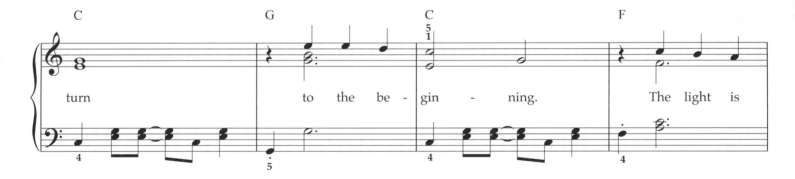

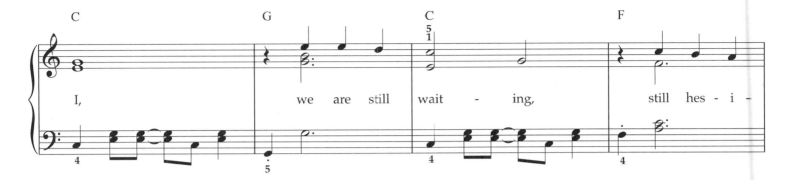

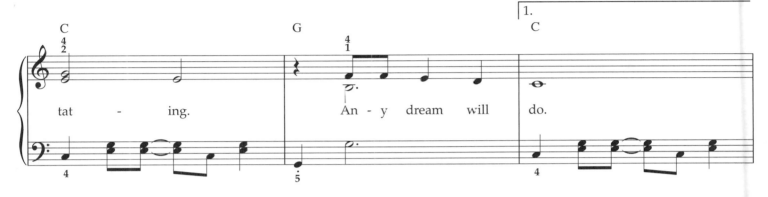

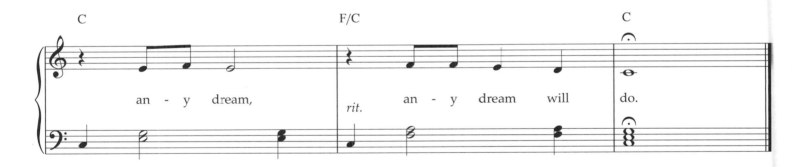

Additional lyrics

2. I wore my coat
    With golden lining,
    Bright colors shining
    Wonderful and new.
    And in the east
    The dawn was breaking,
    And the world was waking
    Any dream will do.

Beauty And The Beast
from Walt Disney's *BEAUTY AND THE BEAST: THE BROADWAY MUSICAL*

Lyrics by Howard Ashman
Music by Alan Menken

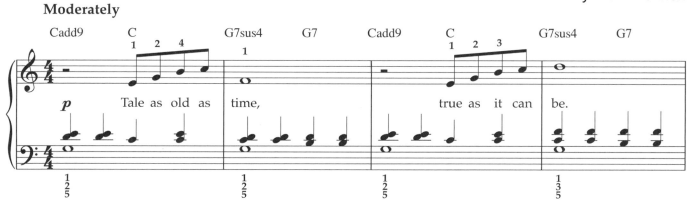

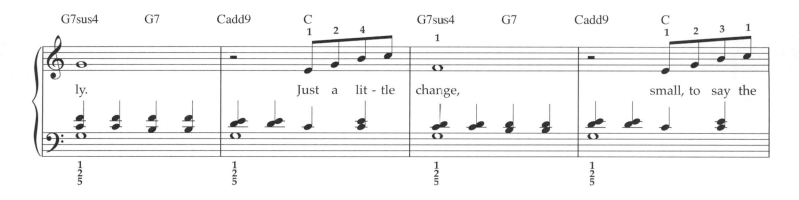

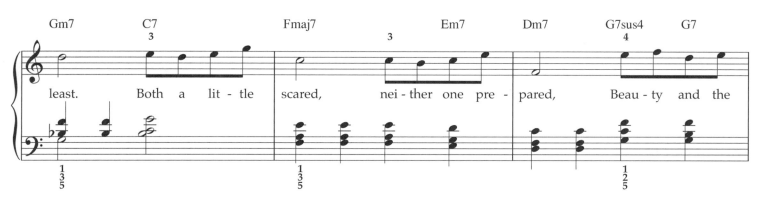

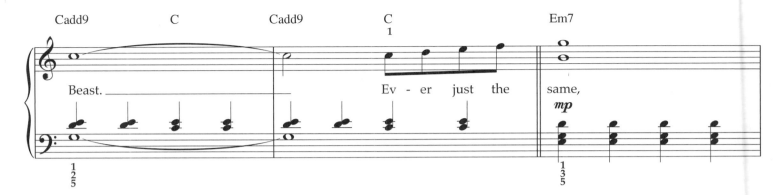

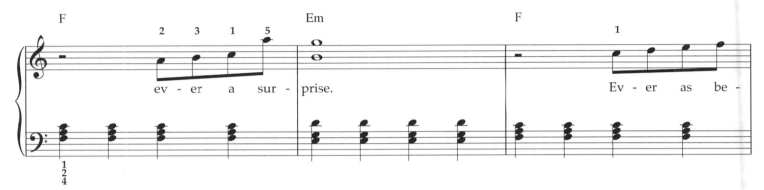

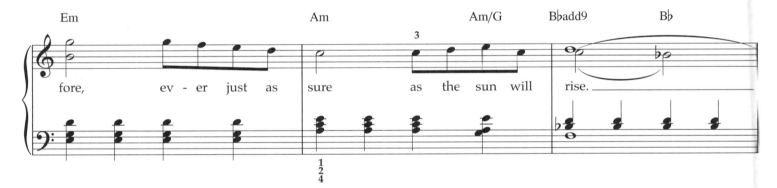

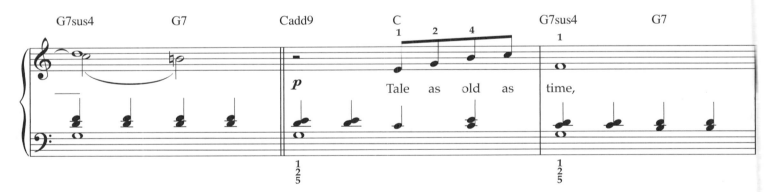

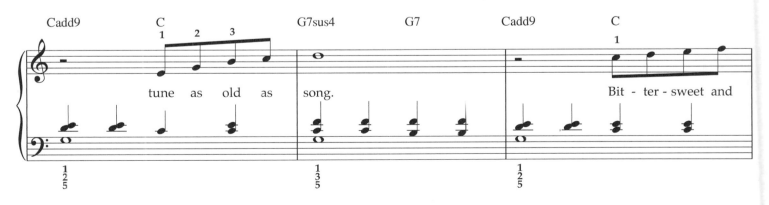

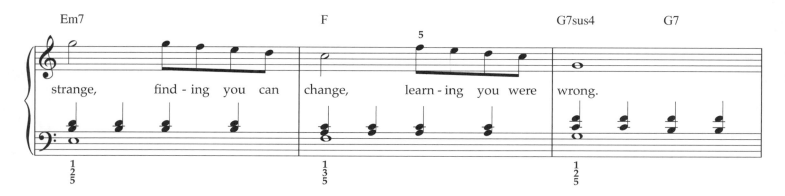

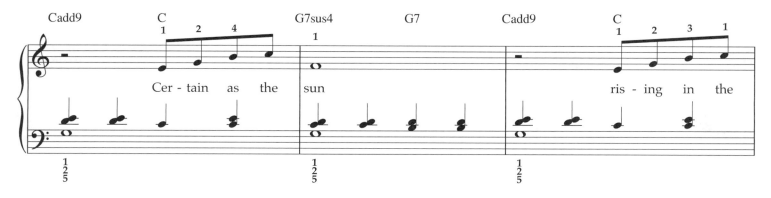

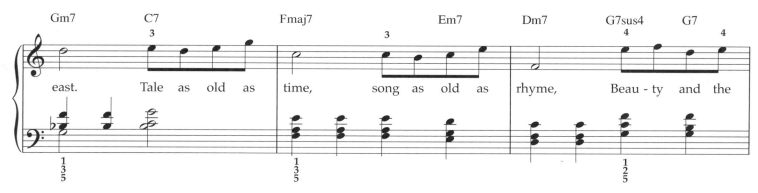

Slower

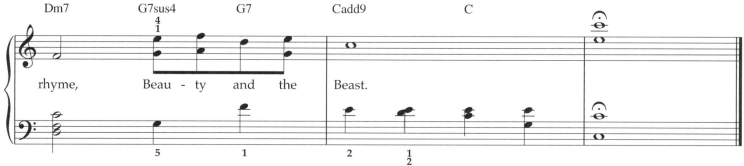

Do-Re-Mi
from *THE SOUND OF MUSIC*

Lyrics by Oscar Hammerstein II
Music by Richard Rodgers

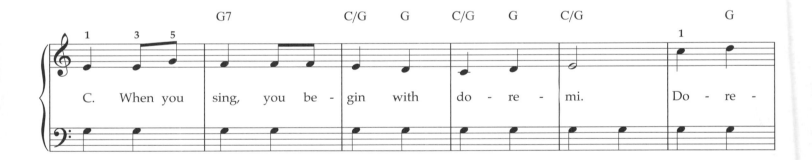

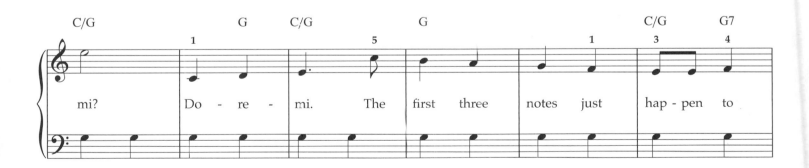

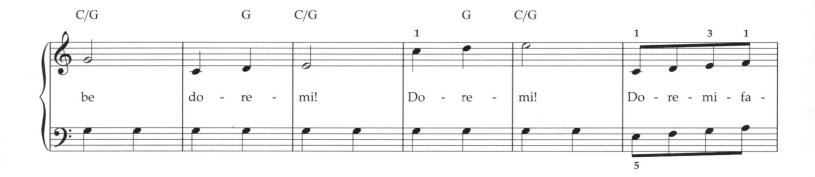

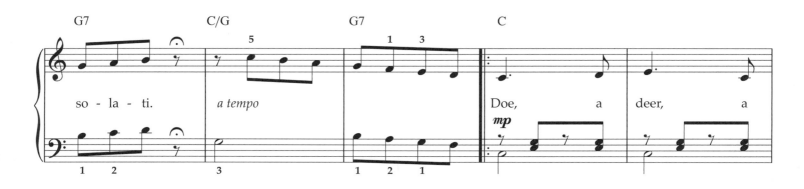

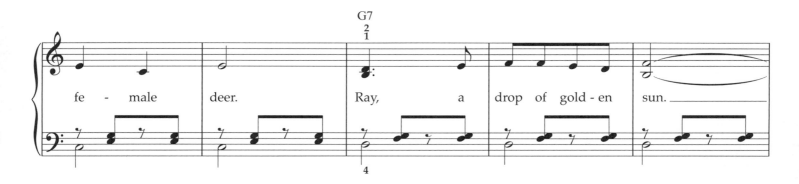

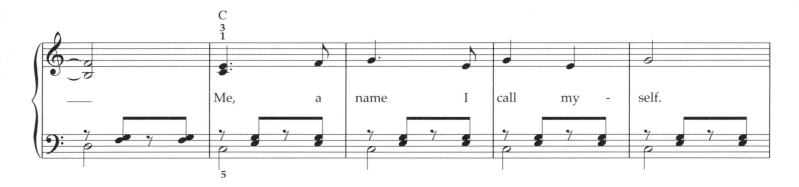

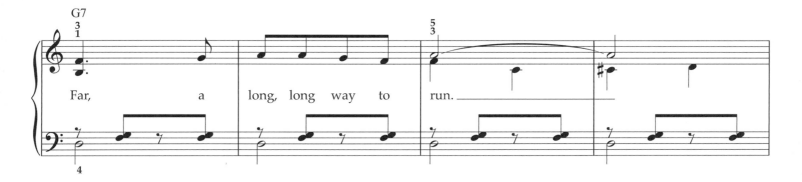

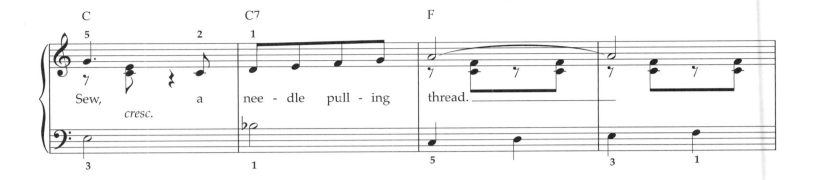

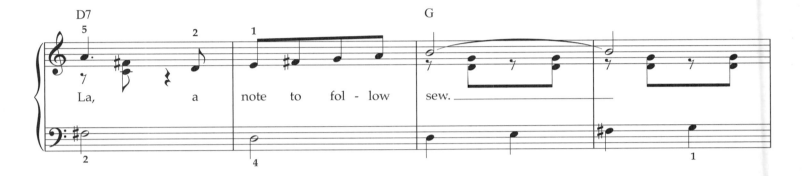

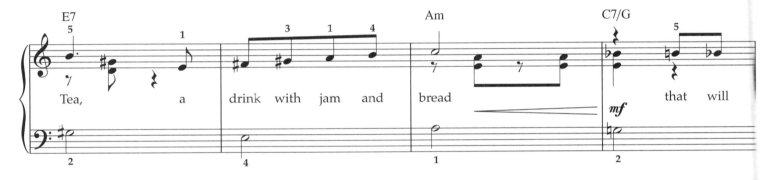

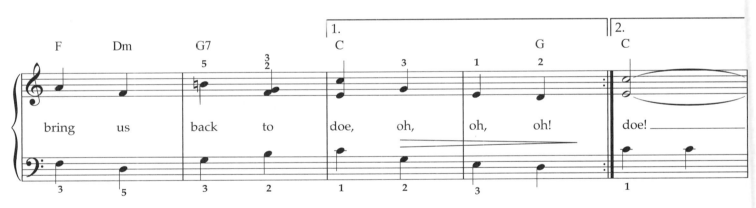

Consider Yourself

from the Broadway musical *OLIVER!*

Words and Music by Lionel Bart

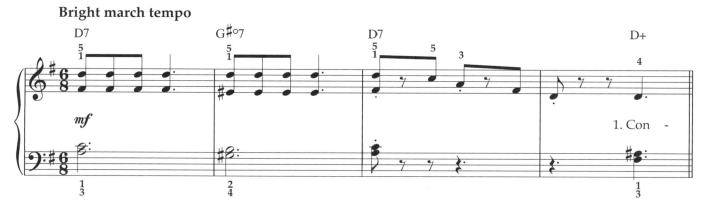

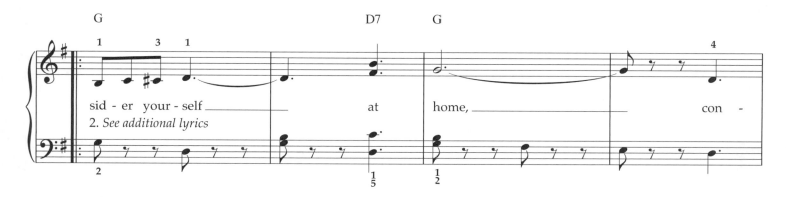

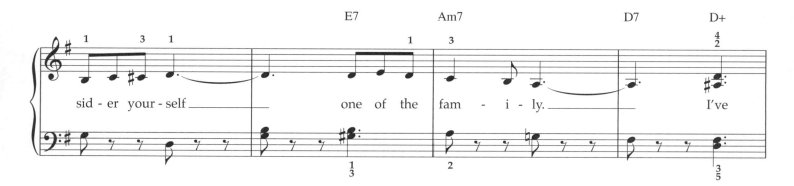

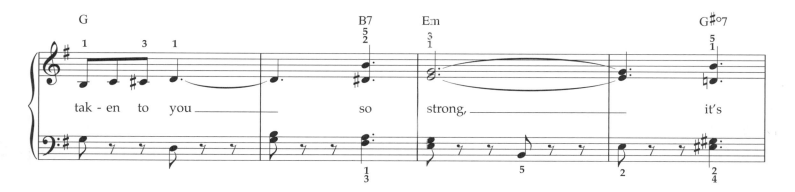

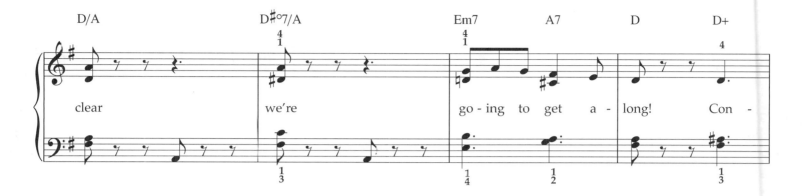

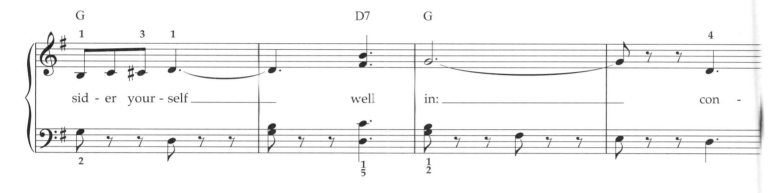

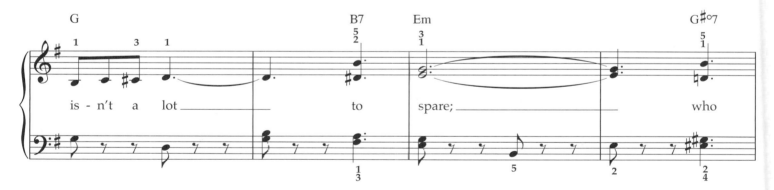

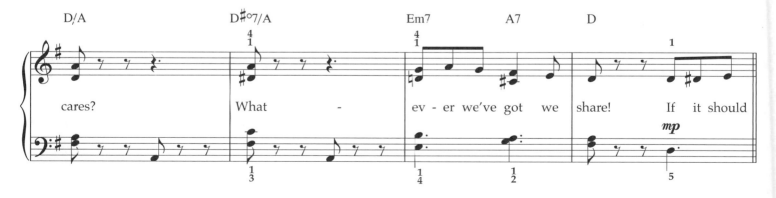

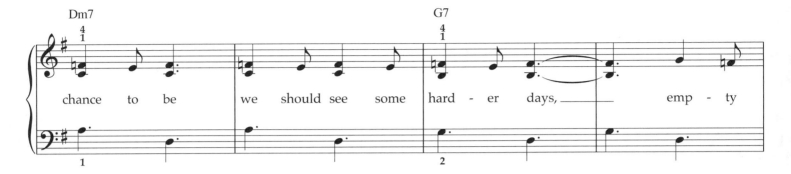

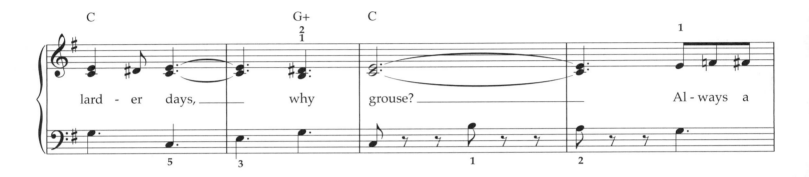

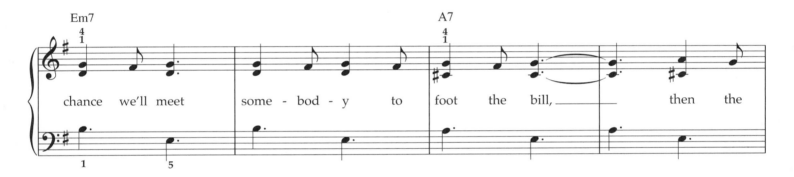

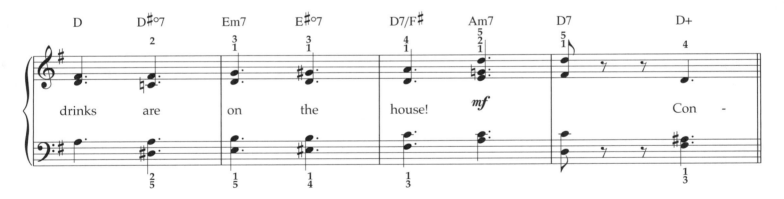

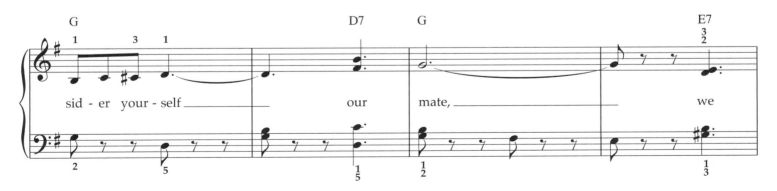

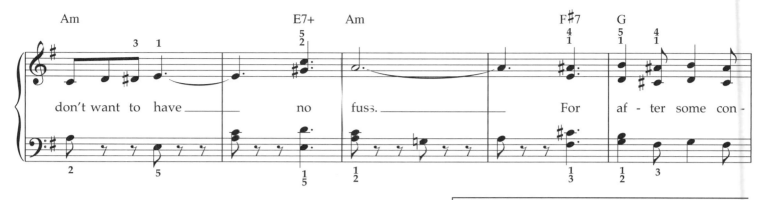

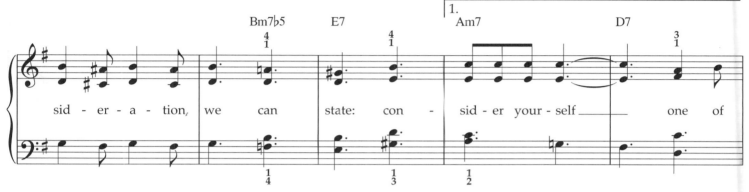

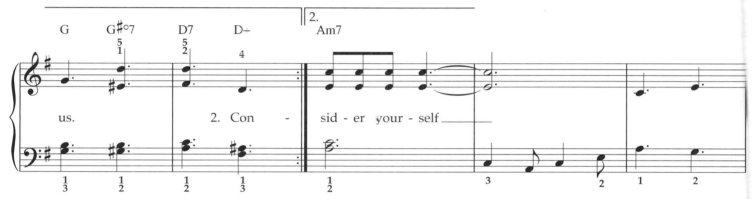

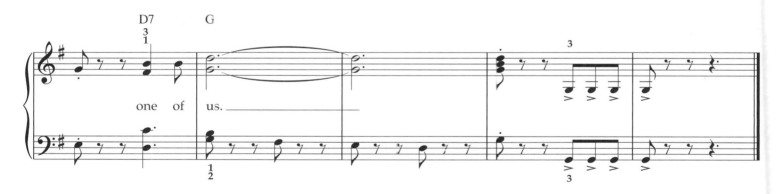

Additional lyrics

2. Consider yourself at home,
   Consider yourself one of the family.
   We've taken to you so strong,
   It's clear we're going to get along!
   Consider yourself well in:
   Consider yourself part of the furniture.
   There isn't a lot to spare;
   Who cares? Whatever we've got we share!

Nobody tries to be lah-di-dah and uppity,
There's a cup o' tea for all.
Only it's wise to be handy wiv a rolling pin
When the landlord comes to call!
Consider yourself our mate,
We don't want to have no fuss.
For after some consideration we can state:
Consider yourself one of us.

Hello, Dolly!

from *HELLO, DOLLY!*

Music and Lyric by Jerry Herman

Moderately

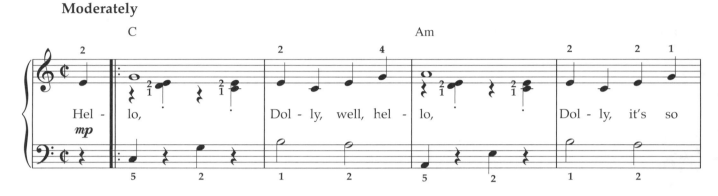

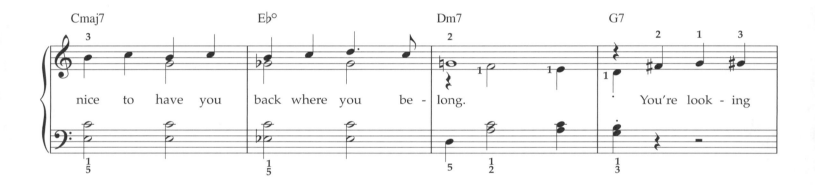

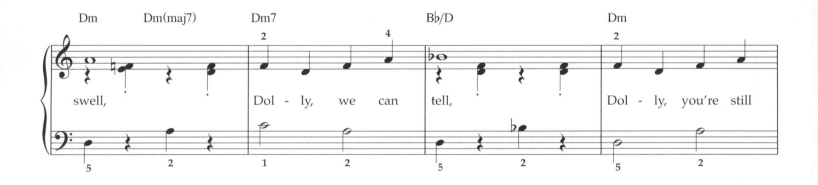

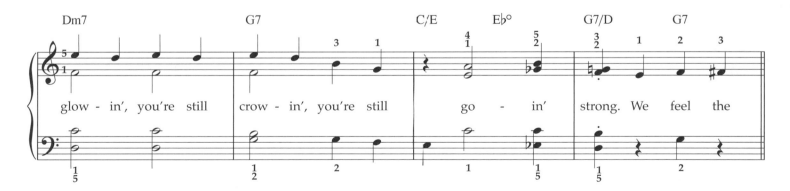

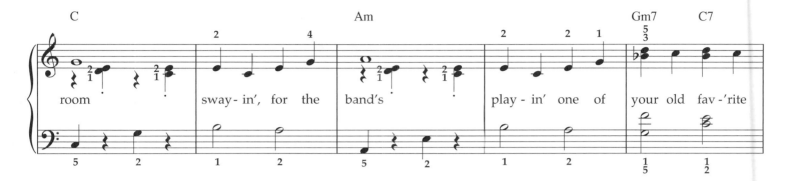

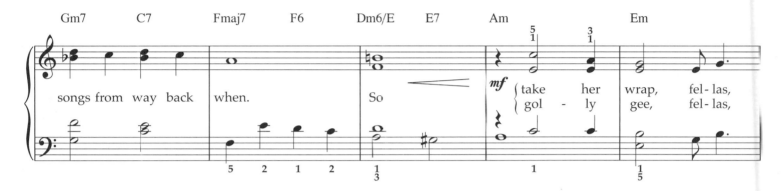

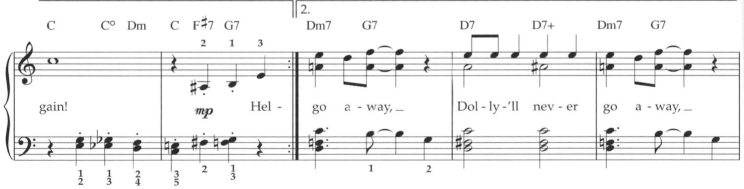

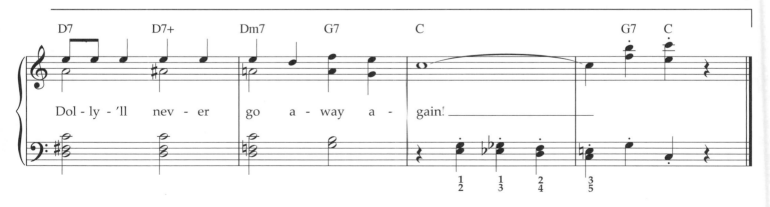

I Dreamed A Dream
from *LES MISÉRABLES*

Music by Claude-Michel Schönberg
Lyrics by Alain Boublil, Jean-Marc Natel and Herbert Kretzmer

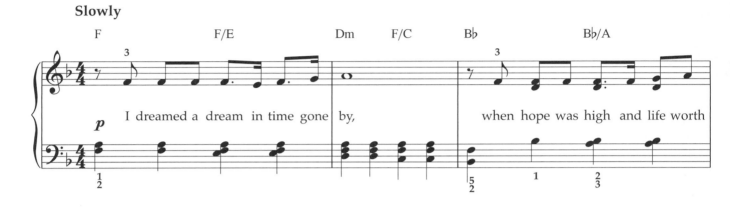

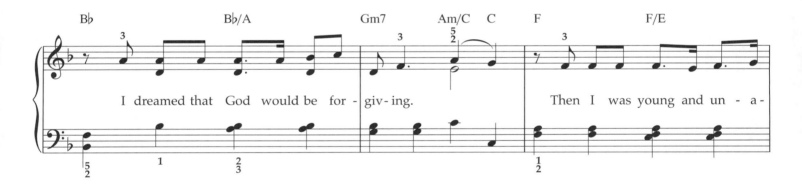

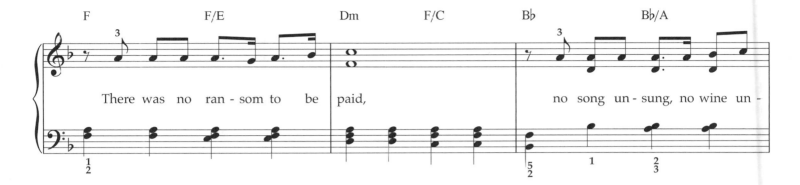

There was no ran-som to be paid, no song un-sung, no wine un -

tast-ed. But the ti-gers come at night, with their voic-es soft as

thun - der. _____ As they tear your hope a - part,

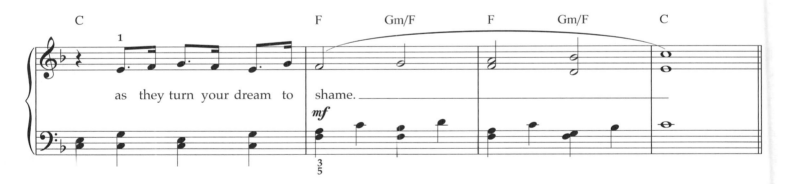

as they turn your dream to shame. _____

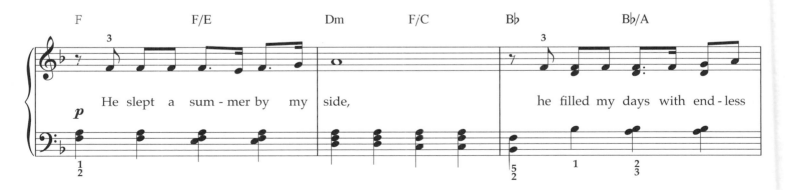

He slept a sum-mer by my side, he filled my days with end-less

wonder.
He took my child-hood in his stride,

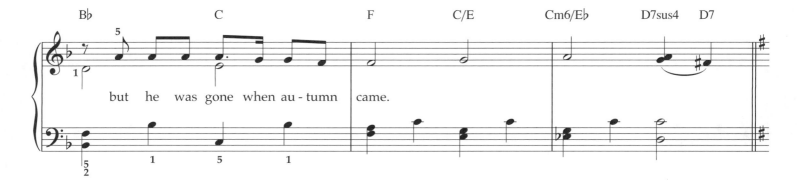

but he was gone when au-tumn came.

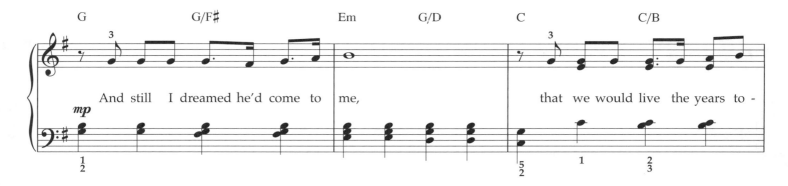

And still I dreamed he'd come to me,
that we would live the years to-

geth-er.
But there are dreams that can-not be,

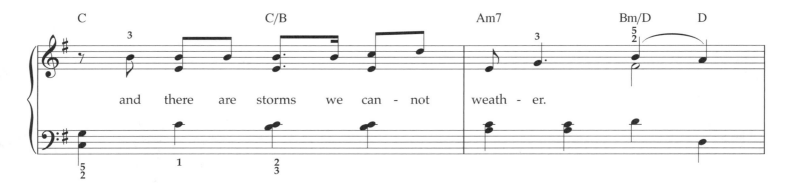

and there are storms we can-not weath-er.

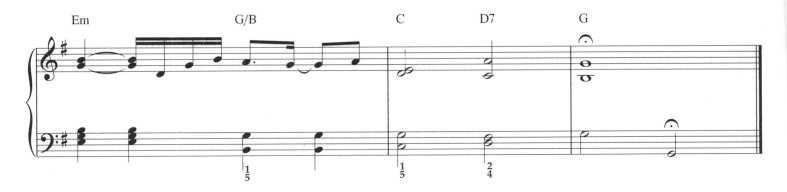

It Might As Well Be Spring

from *STATE FAIR*

Lyrics by Oscar Hammerstein II
Music by Richard Rodgers

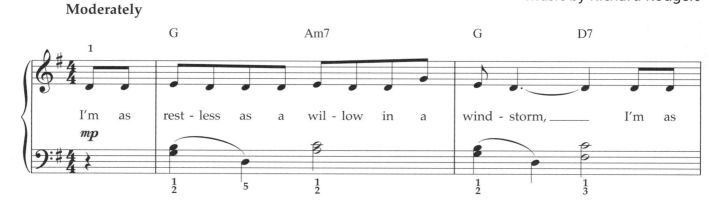

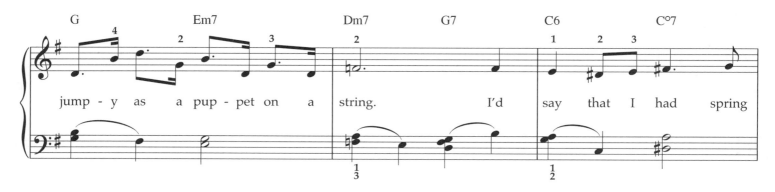

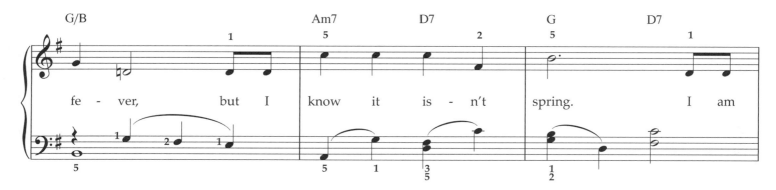

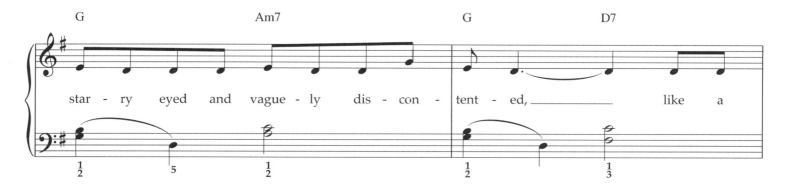

27

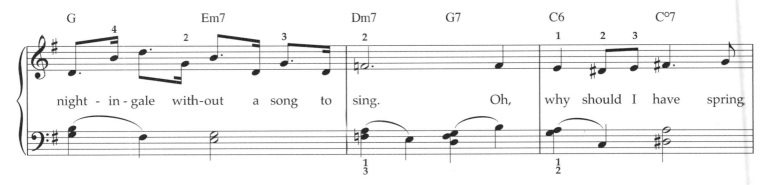

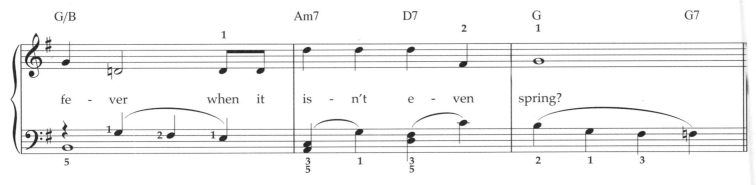

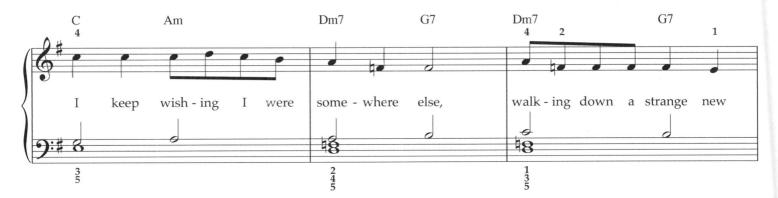

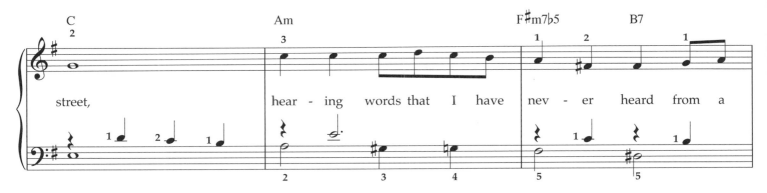

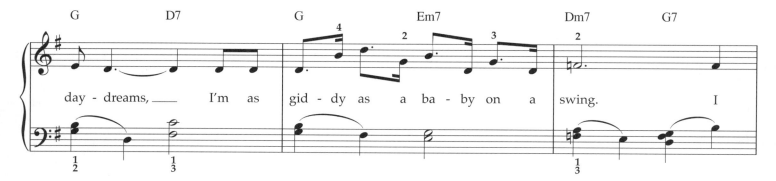

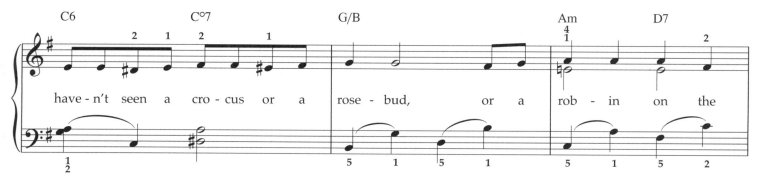

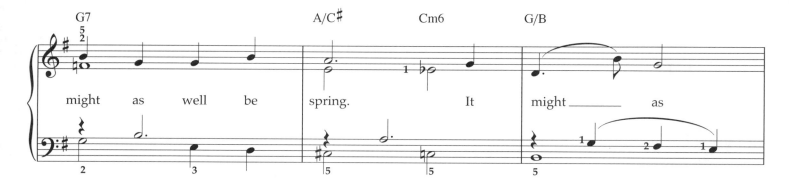

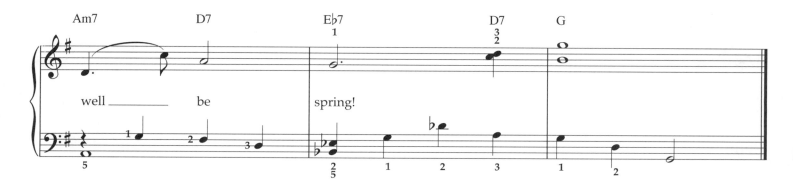

Don't Cry For Me Argentina

from *EVITA*

Words by Tim Rice
Music by Andrew Lloyd Webber

Moderately slow

I had to let it hap-pen, I had to change; Could-n't

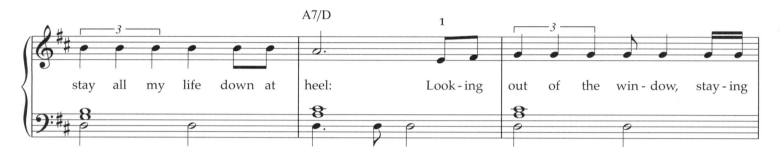

stay all my life down at heel: Look-ing out of the win-dow, stay-ing

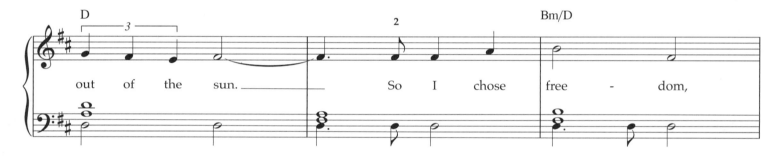

out of the sun. _____ So I chose free - dom,

run - ning a - round try - ing ev - 'ry - thing new, but noth - ing im - pressed me at

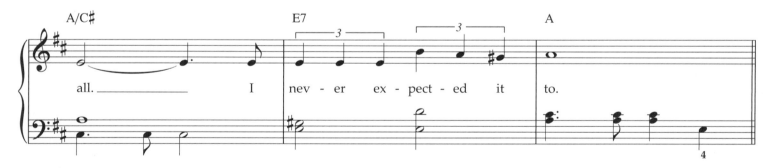

all. _____ I nev - er ex - pect - ed it to.

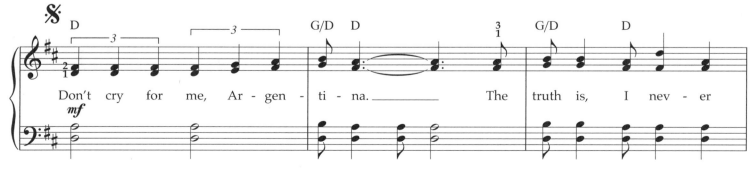

Don't cry for me, Ar - gen - ti - na. _____ The truth is, I nev - er

Additional lyrics

2. And as for fortune and as for fame —
   I never invited them in:
   Though it seemed to the world they were all I desired.
   They are illusions, they're not the solutions they promised to be,
   The answer was here all the time.

I've Never Been In Love Before

from *GUYS AND DOLLS*

By Frank Loesser

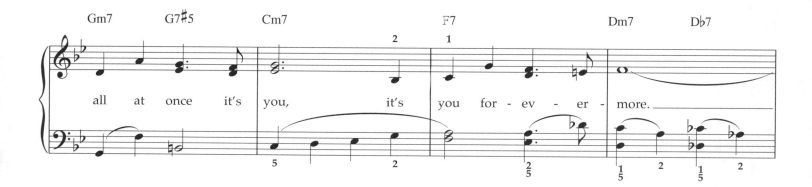

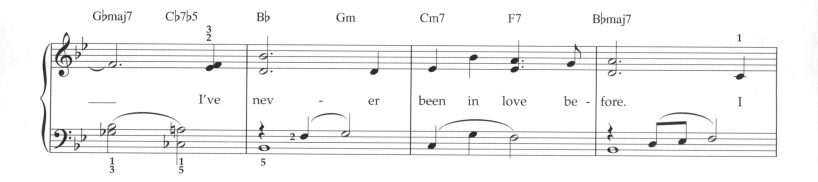

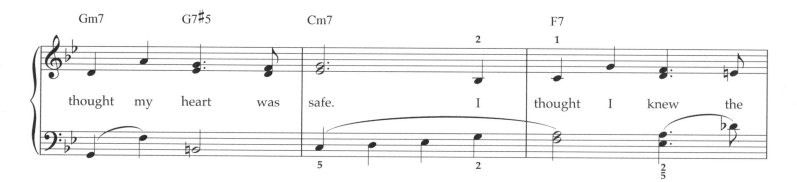

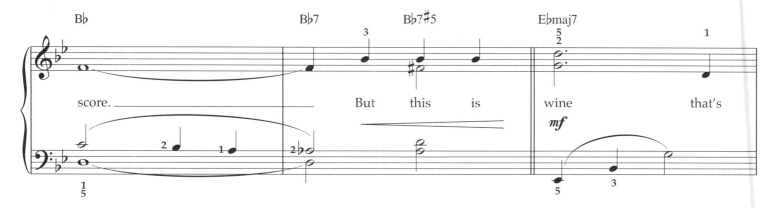

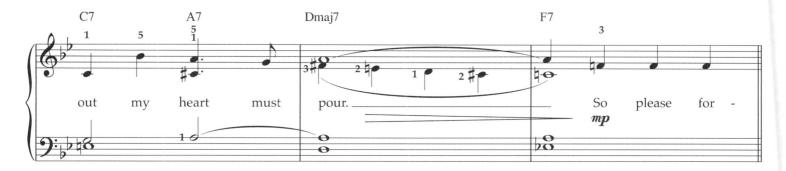

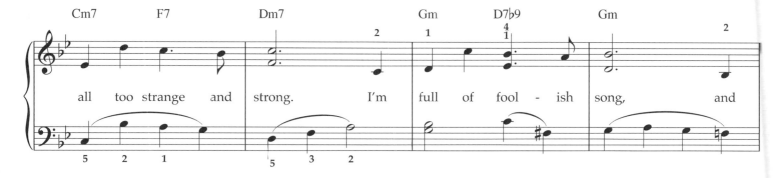

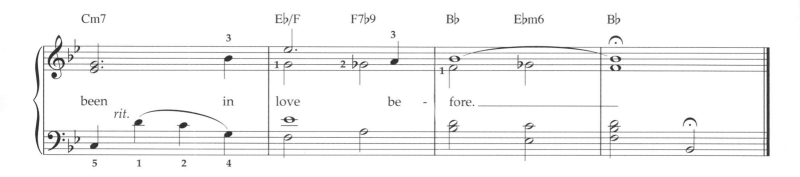

Love Changes Everything

from *ASPECTS OF LOVE*

Music by Andrew Lloyd Webber
Lyrics by Don Black and Charles Hart

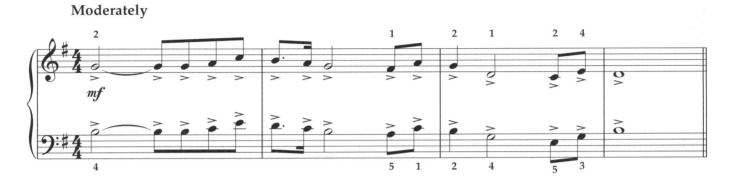

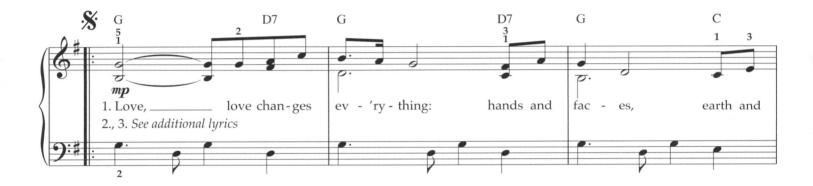

1. Love, _____ love chan-ges ev-'ry-thing: hands and fac-es, earth and
2., 3. *See additional lyrics*

sky. Love, _____ love chan-ges ev-'ry-thing: how you

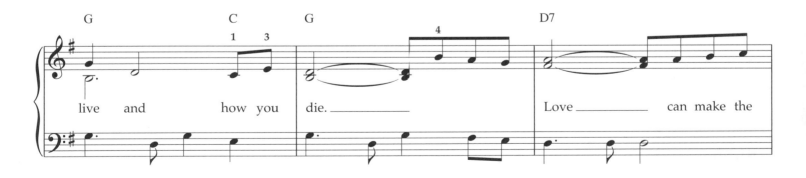

live and how you die. _____ Love _____ can make the

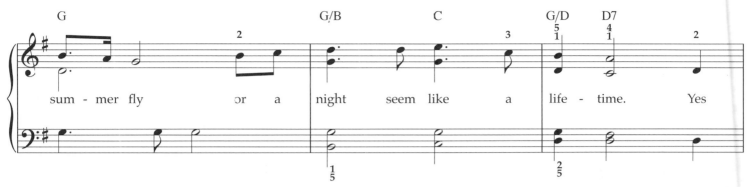

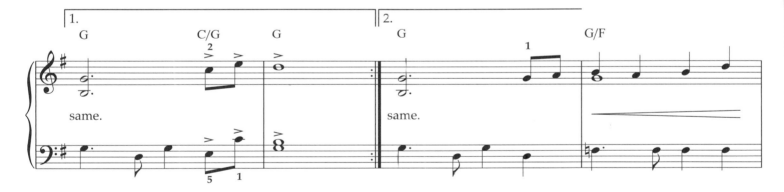

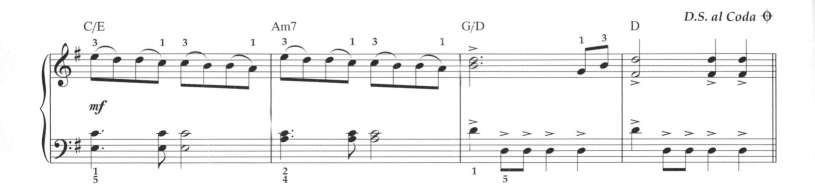

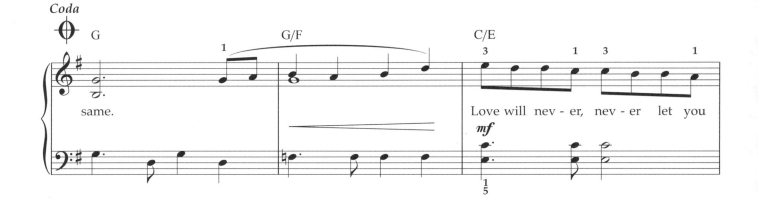

same.

Love will nev - er, nev - er let you

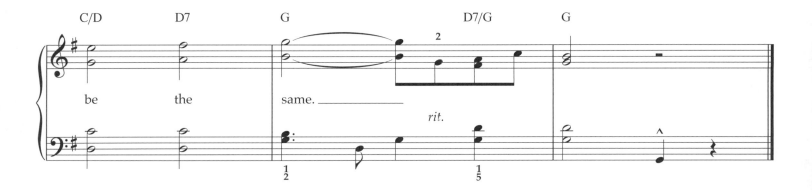

be the same.

rit.

Additional lyrics

2. Love, love changes everything:
   Days are longer, words mean more
   Love, love changes everything:
   Pain is deeper than before.
   Love will turn your world around,
   And that world will last forever.
   Yes love, love changes everything;
   Brings you glory, brings you shame.
   Nothing in this world will ever be the same.

3. Off into the world we go;
   Planning futures shaping years.
   Love bursts in and suddenly,
   All our wisdom disappears.
   Love makes fools of everyone;
   All the rules we make are broken.
   Yes love, love changes everyone;
   Live or perish in its flame.
   Love will never, never let you be the same.
   Love will never, never let you be the same.

I Don't Know How To Love Him

from *JESUS CHRIST SUPERSTAR*

Words by Tim Rice
Music by Andrew Lloyd Webber

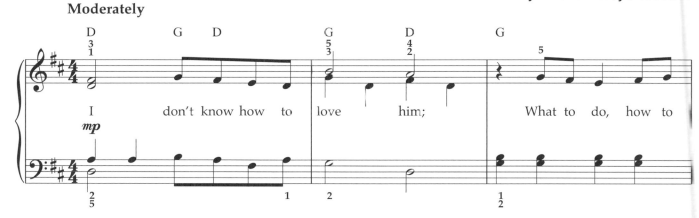

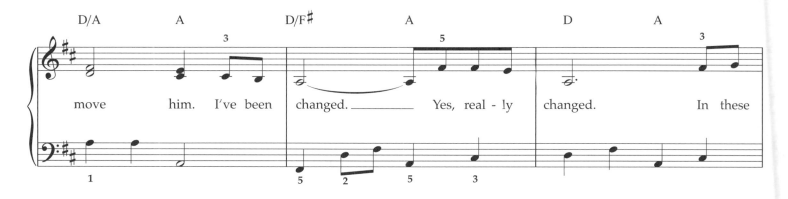

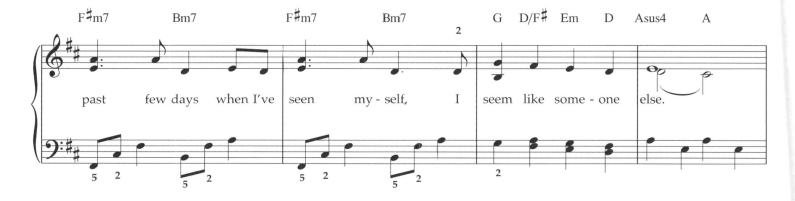

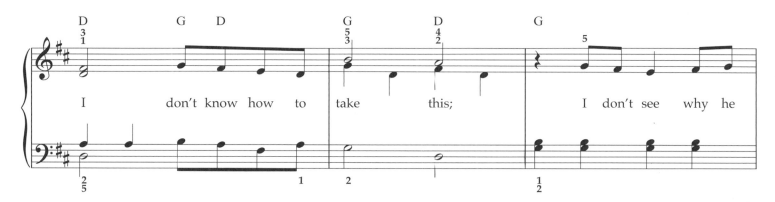

moves me. He's a man._____ He's just a man. And I've

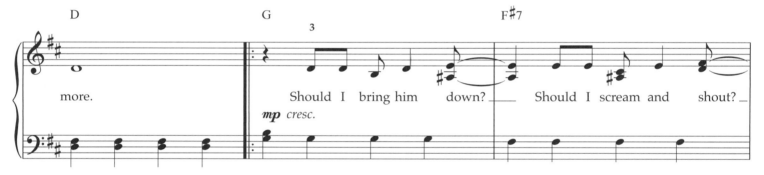

had so man-y men be-fore, in ver-y man-y ways.____ He's just one

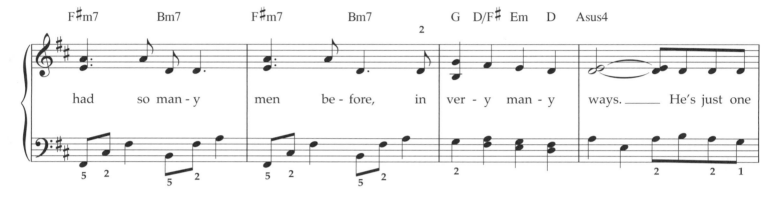

more. Should I bring him down?____ Should I scream and shout?____

____ Should I speak of love?____ Let my feel-ings out?____ I nev-er thought I'd

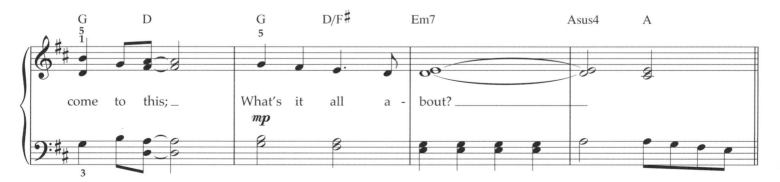

come to this;_ What's it all a-bout?_____

Additional lyrics

2. Yet, if he said he loved me
   I'd be lost, I'd be frightened,
   I couldn't cope,
   Just couldn't cope.
   I'd turn my head, I'd back away,
   I wouldn't want to know.
   He scares me so.
   I want him so.
   I love him so.

The Lady Is A Tramp

from *BABES IN ARMS*
from *WORDS AND MUSIC*

Words by Lorenz Hart
Music by Richard Rodgers

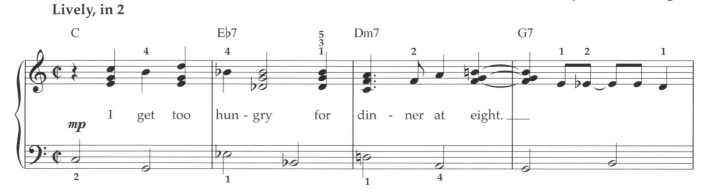

I get too hun - gry for din - ner at eight.

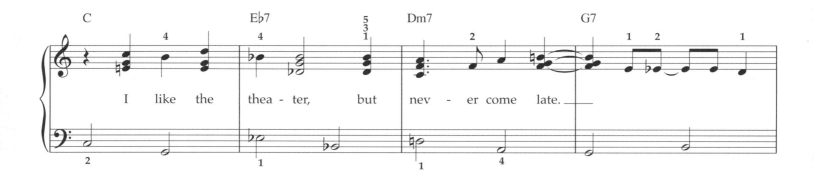

I like the thea - ter, but nev - er come late.

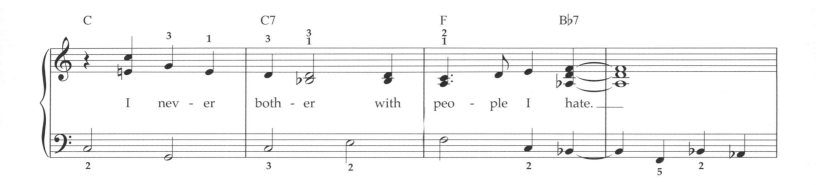

I nev - er both - er with peo - ple I hate.

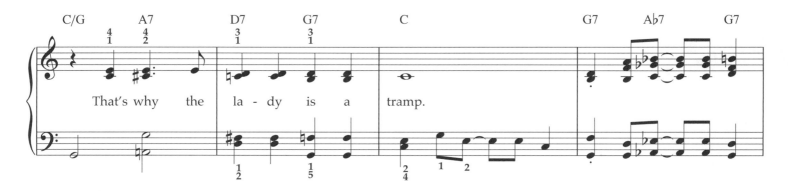

That's why the la - dy is a tramp.

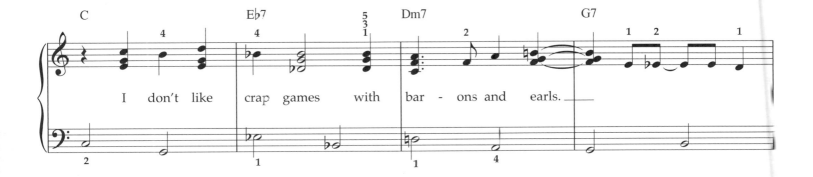

I don't like crap games with bar - ons and earls.

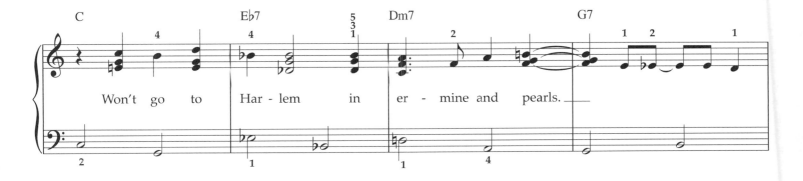

Won't go to Har - lem in er - mine and pearls.

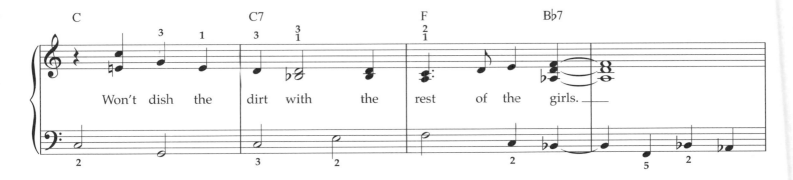

Won't dish the dirt with the rest of the girls.

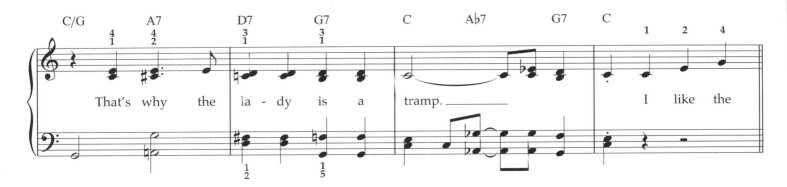

That's why the la - dy is a tramp. I like the

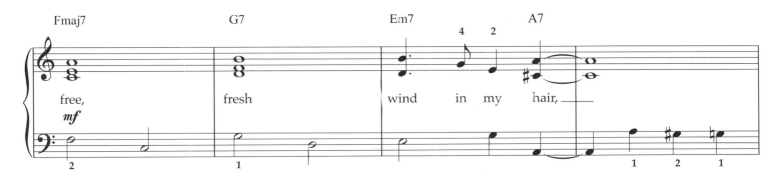

free, fresh wind in my hair,

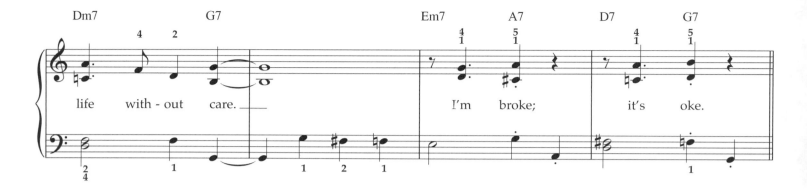

life with - out care. ___ I'm broke; it's oke.

Hate Cal - i - for - nia, it's cold and it's damp. ___

___ That's why the la - dy is a

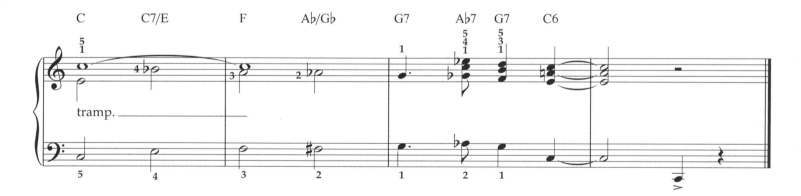

tramp. ___

Leaning On A Lamp Post

from *ME AND MY GIRL*

By Noel Gay

Moderately, with a swing

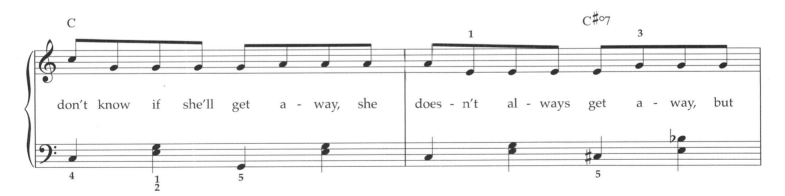

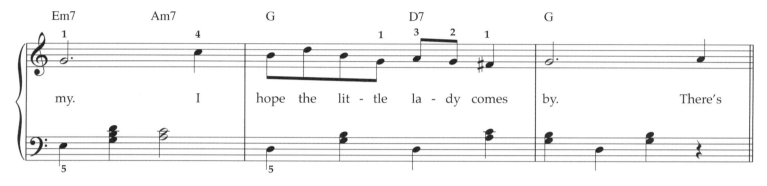

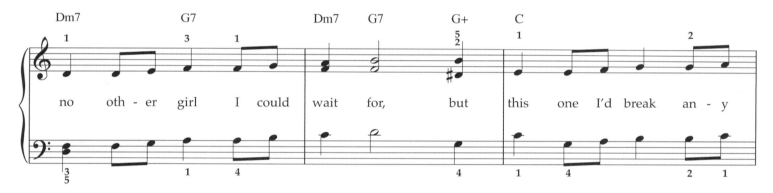

absolutely wonderful and marvelous and beautiful, and

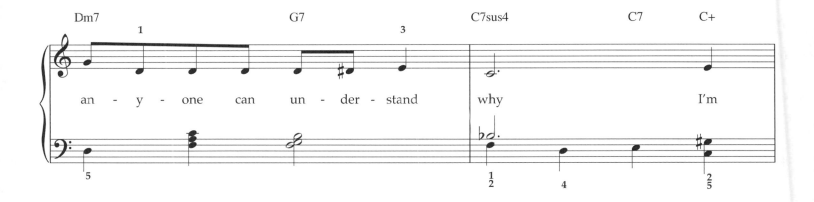

an-y-one can understand why I'm

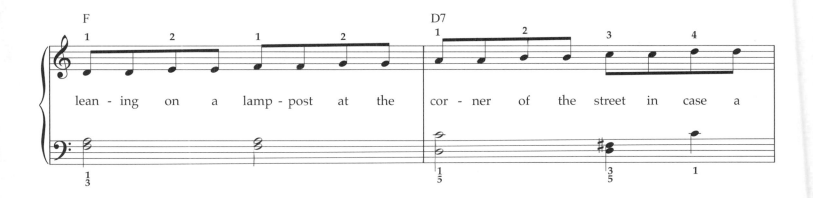

lean-ing on a lamp-post at the cor-ner of the street in case a

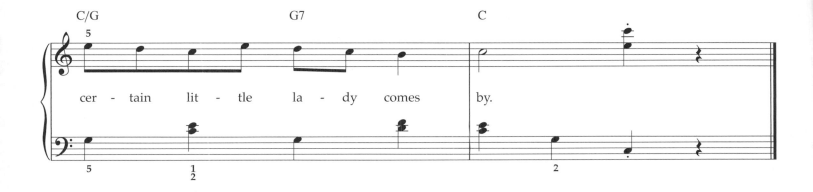

cer-tain lit-tle la-dy comes by.

Mamma Mia
from *MAMMA MIA!*

Words and Music by
Benny Andersson, Bjorn Ulvaeus and Stig Anderson

Moderately fast, with a driving beat

1. I was cheat-ed by you and I think you know when.
2. *See additional lyrics*

So I made up my mind it must come to an end.

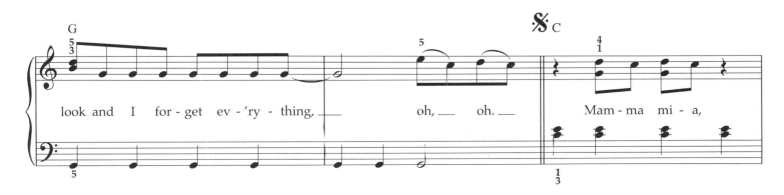

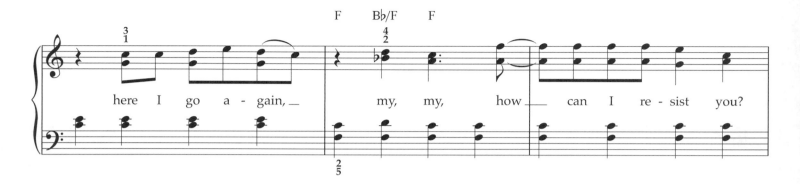

here I go a-gain, __ my, my, how __ can I re-sist you?

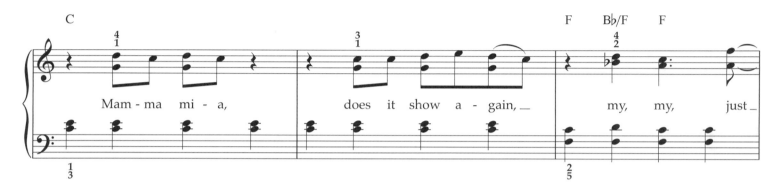

Mam-ma mi-a, does it show a-gain, __ my, my, just __

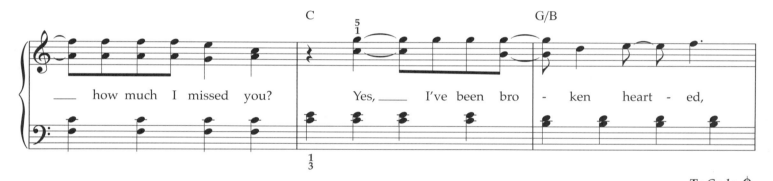

__ how much I missed you? Yes, __ I've been bro- ken heart-ed,

To Coda

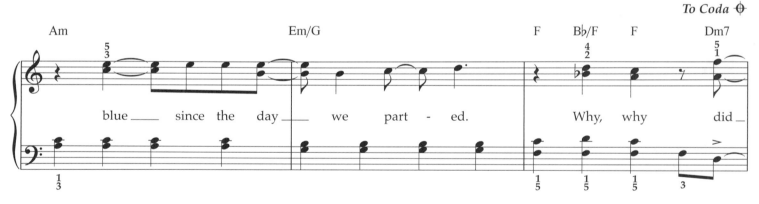

blue __ since the day __ we part-ed. Why, why did __

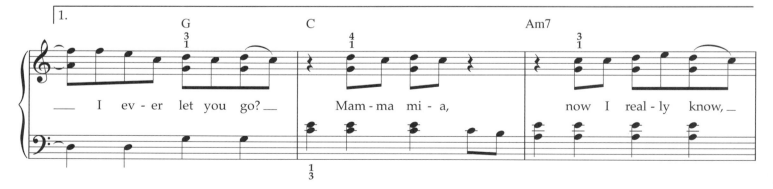

__ I ev-er let you go? __ Mam-ma mi-a, now I real-ly know, __

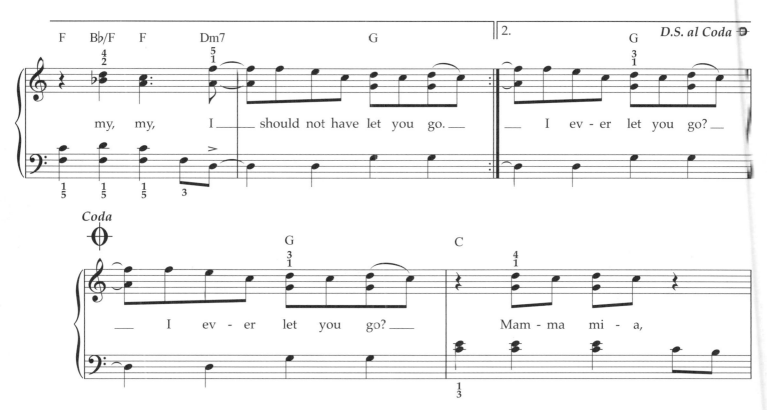

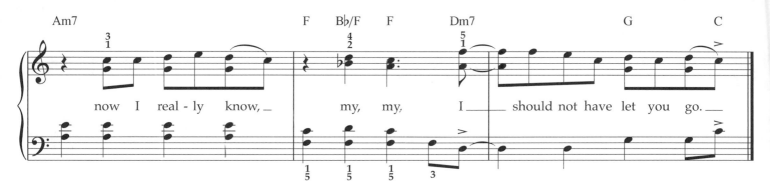

Additional lyrics

2. I was angry and sad when I knew we were through.
I can't count all the times I have cried over you.
Look at me now, will I ever learn?
I don't know how, but I suddenly lose control.
There's a fire within my soul.
Just one look and I can hear a bell ring.
One more look and I forget everything, oh, oh.

Memory

from *CATS*

Music by Andrew Lloyd Webber
Text by Trevor Nunn after T.S. Eliot

Slowly

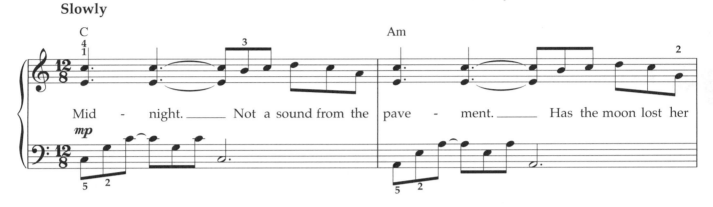

Mid - night. _____ Not a sound from the pave - ment. _____ Has the moon lost her

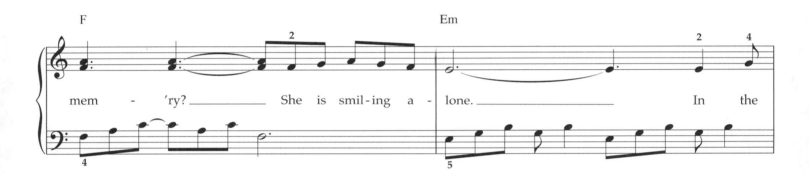

mem - 'ry? _____ She is smil-ing a - lone. _____ In the

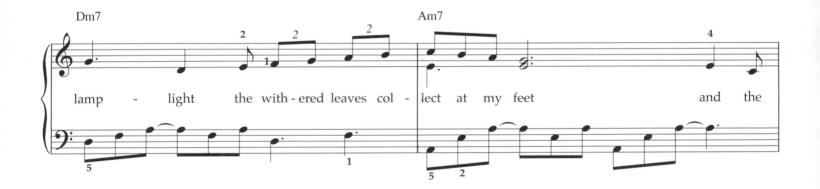

lamp - light the with-ered leaves col - lect at my feet and the

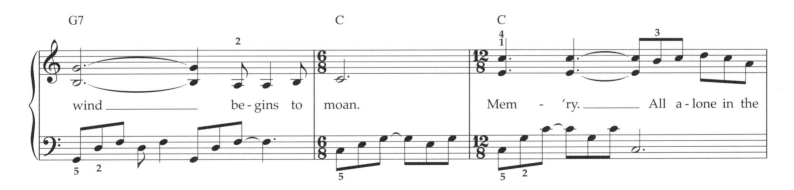

wind _____ be - gins to moan. Mem - 'ry. _____ All a - lone in the

moon - light, _____ I can smile at the old days, _____ I was beau - ti - ful

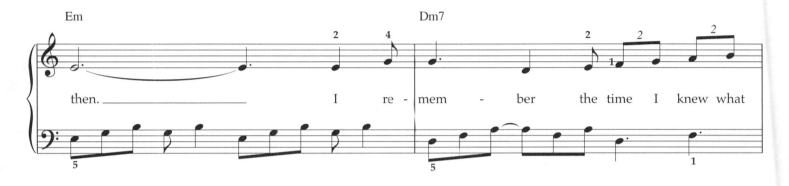

then. _____ I re - mem - ber the time I knew what

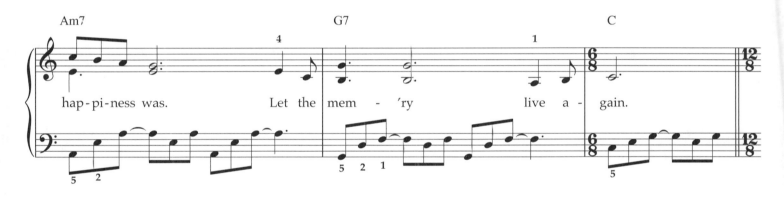

hap - pi - ness was. Let the mem - 'ry live a - gain.

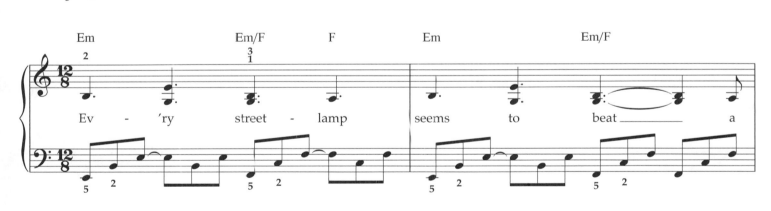

Ev - 'ry street - lamp seems to beat _____ a

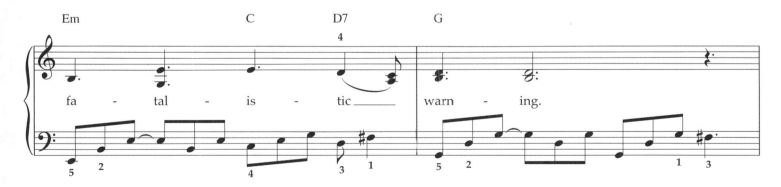

fa - tal - is - tic _____ warn - ing.

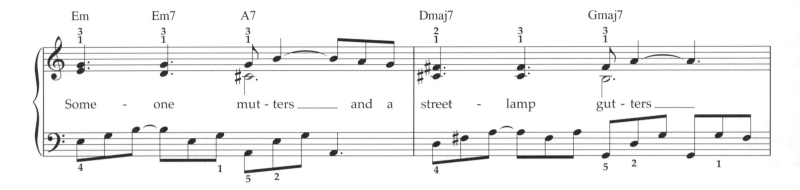

Some - one mut - ters _____ and a street - lamp gut - ters _____

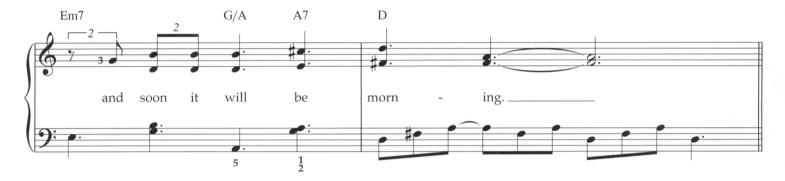

and soon it will be morn - ing. _____

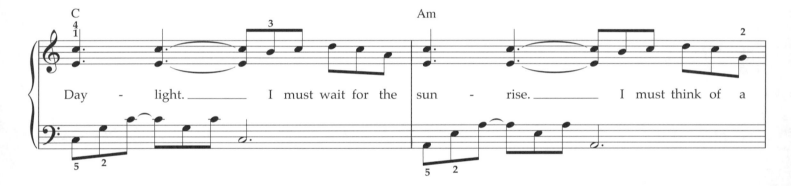

Day - light. _____ I must wait for the sun - rise. _____ I must think of a

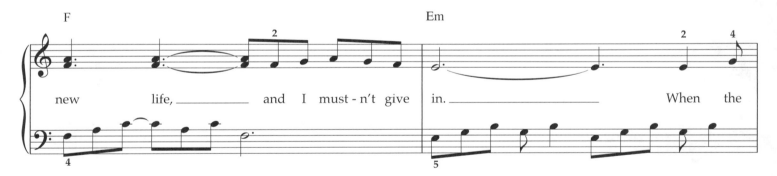

new life, _____ and I must - n't give in. _____ When the

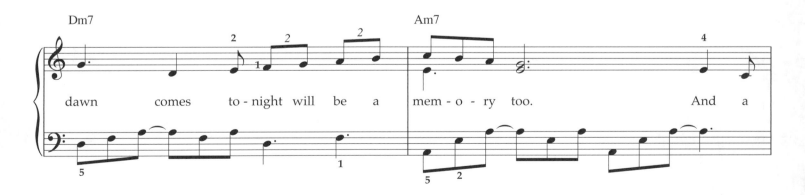

dawn comes to - night will be a mem - o - ry too. And a

new day will be - gin.

Burnt - out ends of smok - y days, _____

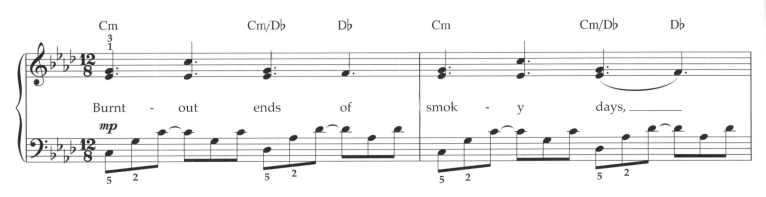

the stale, cold smell of _____ morn - ing. _____ The

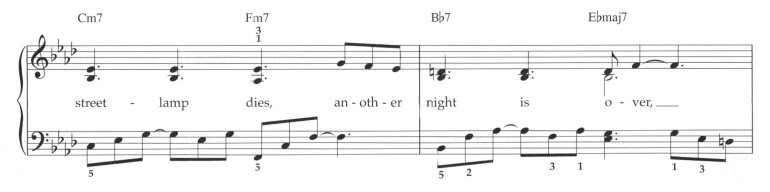

street - lamp dies, an - oth - er night is o - ver, _____

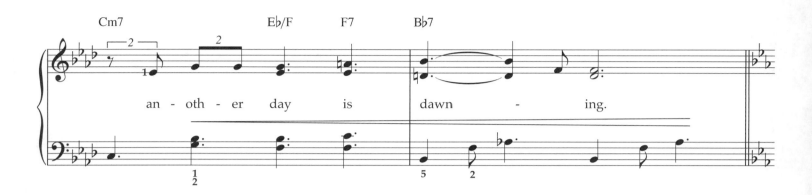

an - oth - er day is dawn - ing.

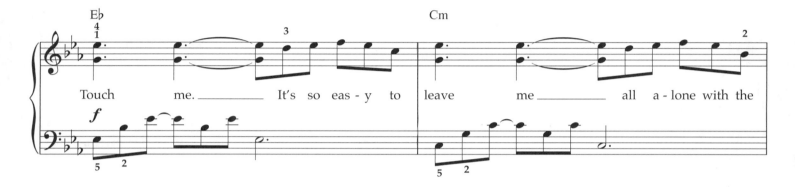

Touch me. It's so eas - y to leave me all a - lone with the

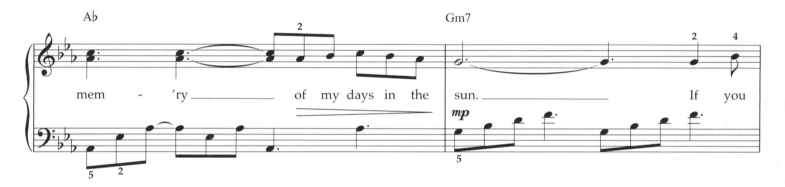

mem - 'ry of my days in the sun. If you

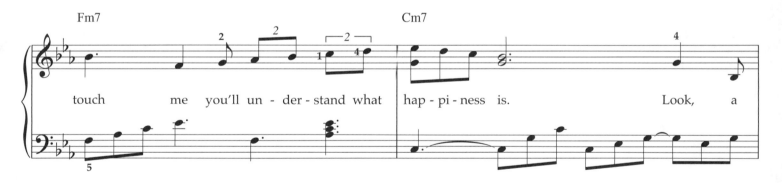

touch me you'll un - der - stand what hap - pi - ness is. Look, a

new day has be - gun.

Never Never Land
from *PETER PAN*

Lyric by Betty Comden and Adolph Green
Music by Jule Styne

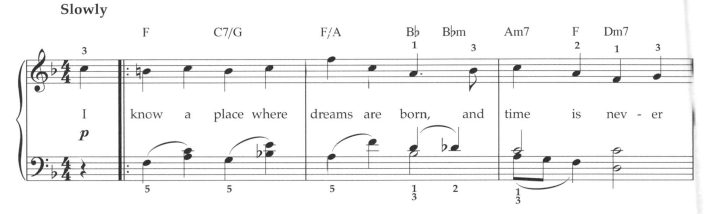

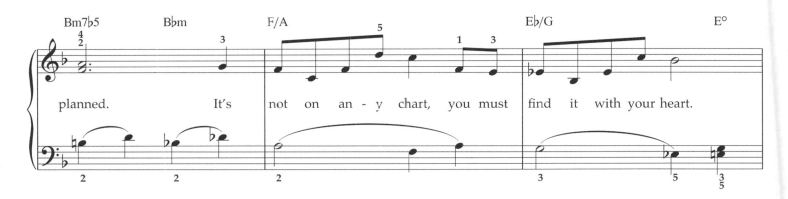

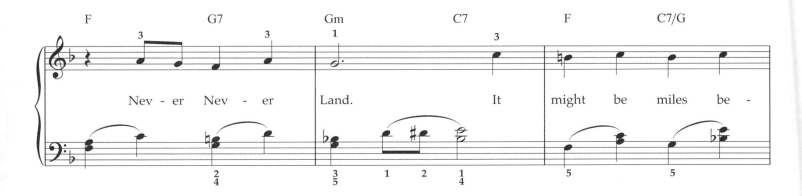

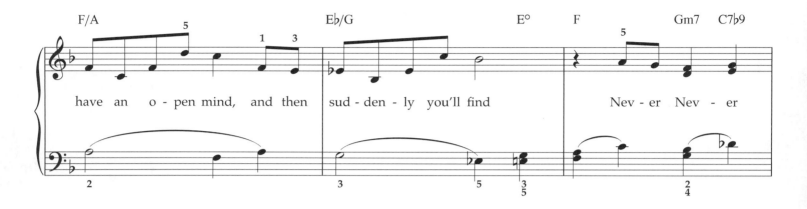

have an o-pen mind, and then sud-den-ly you'll find Nev-er Nev-er

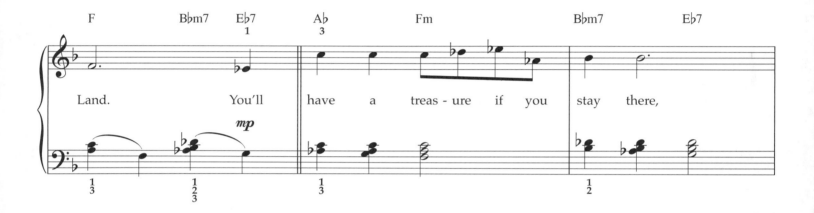

Land. You'll have a treas-ure if you stay there,

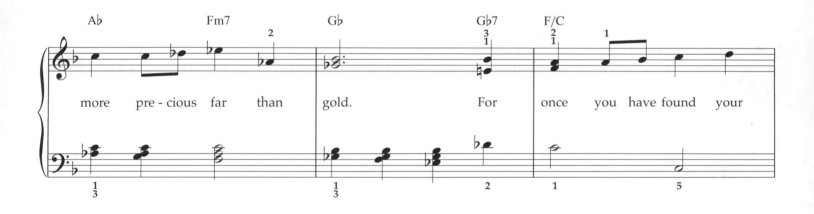

more pre-cious far than gold. For once you have found your

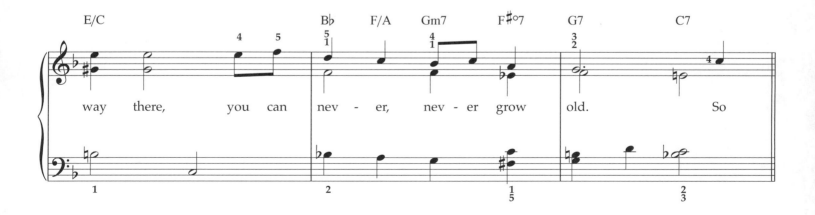

way there, you can nev-er, nev-er grow old. So

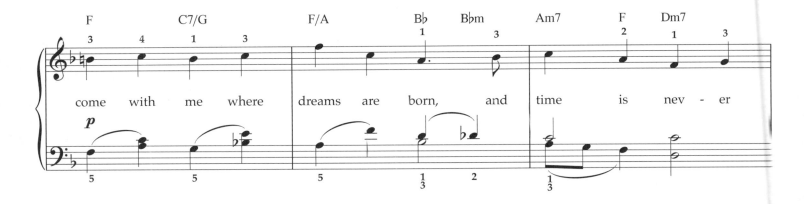

come with me where dreams are born, and time is nev - er

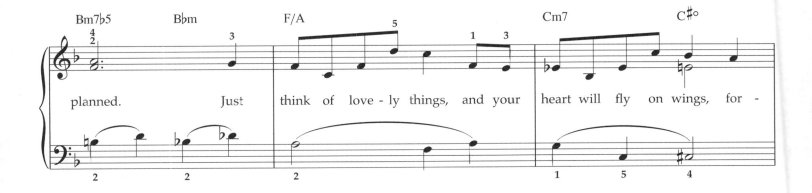

planned. Just think of love - ly things, and your heart will fly on wings, for -

1.

ev - er in Nev - er Nev - er Land _____

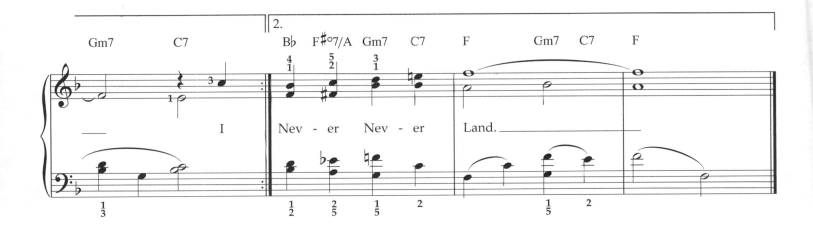

2.

_____ I Nev - er Nev - er Land. _____

One
from *A CHORUS LINE*

Music by Marvin Hamlisch
Lyric by Edward Kleban

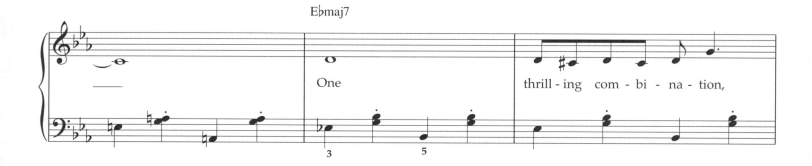

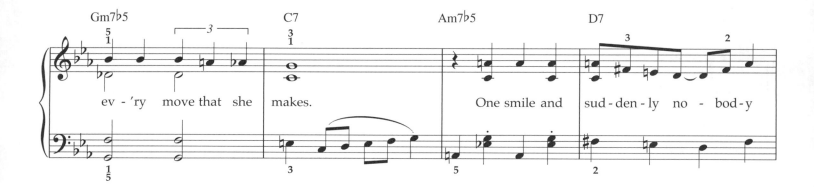

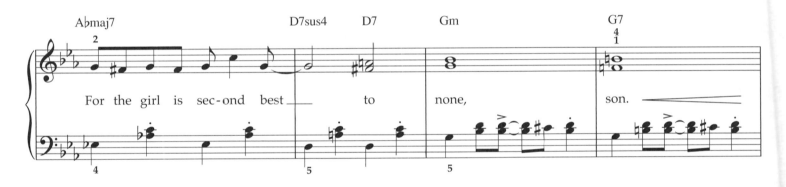

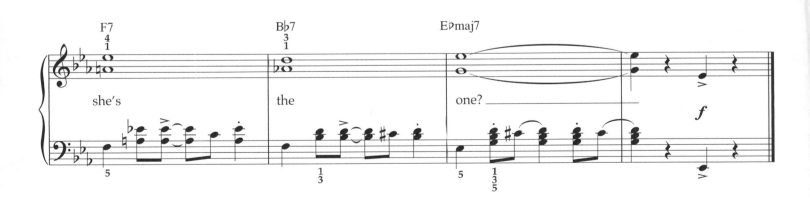

Once Upon A Time
from the Broadway musical ALL AMERICAN

Lyric by Lee Adams
Music by Charles Strouse

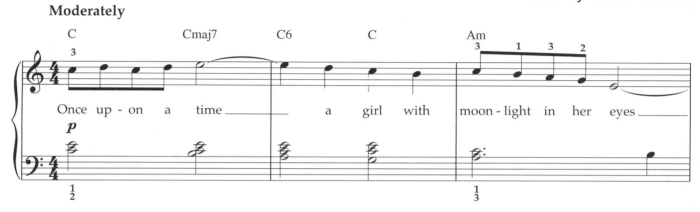

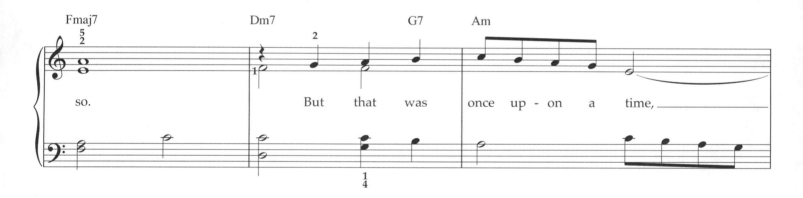

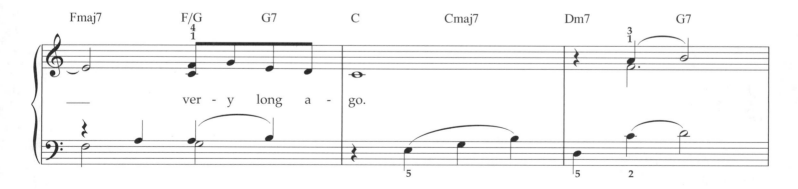

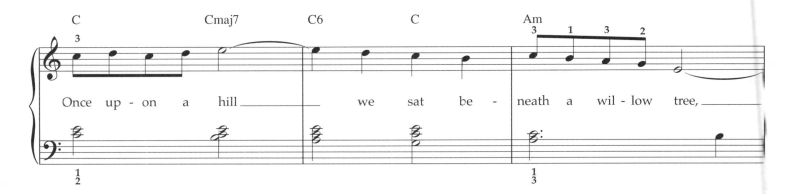

Once up - on a hill ____ we sat be - neath a wil - low tree, ____

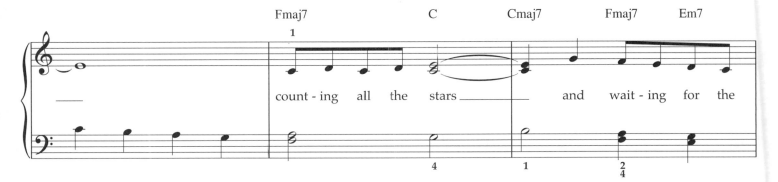

____ count - ing all the stars ____ and wait - ing for the

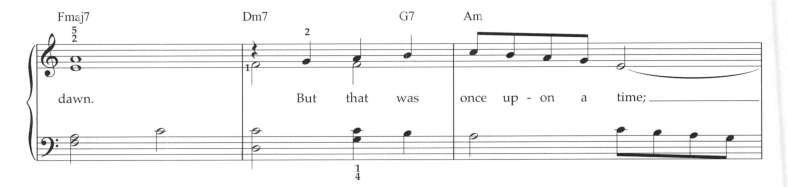

dawn. But that was once up - on a time; ____

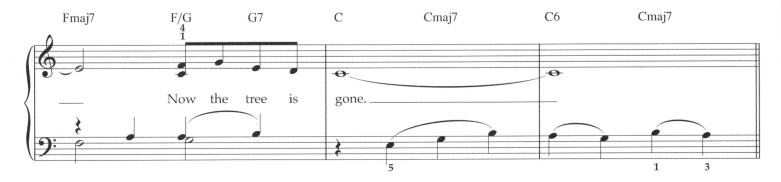

____ Now the tree is gone. ____

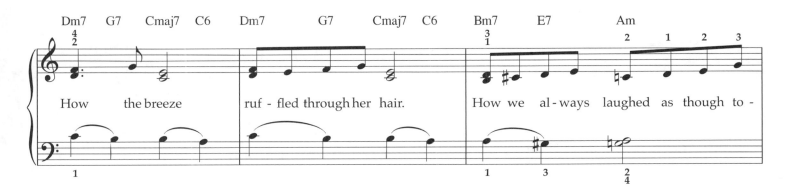

How the breeze ruf - fled through her hair. How we al - ways laughed as though to -

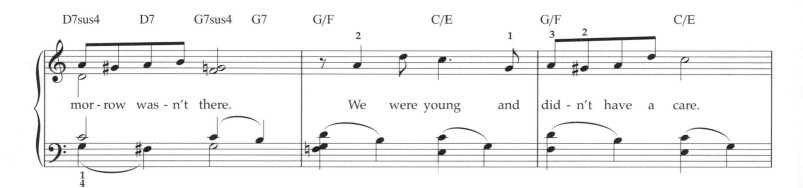

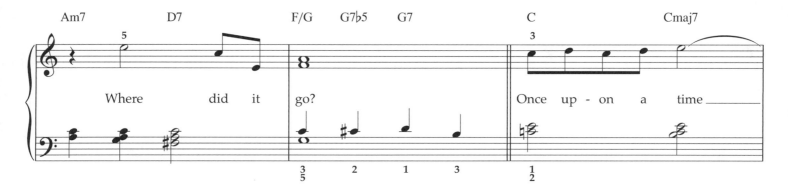

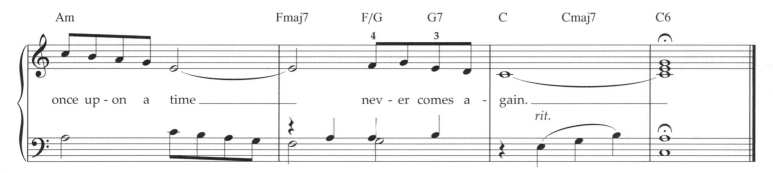

Real Live Girl

from *LITTLE ME*

Music by Cy Coleman
Lyrics by Carolyn Leigh

Moderate Waltz

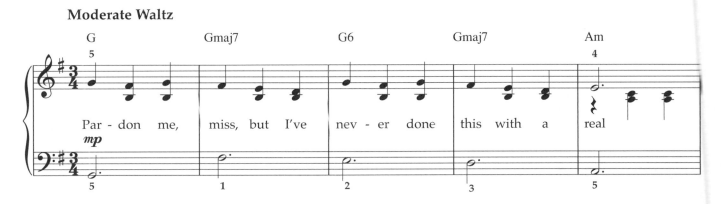

Par-don me, miss, but I've nev-er done this with a real

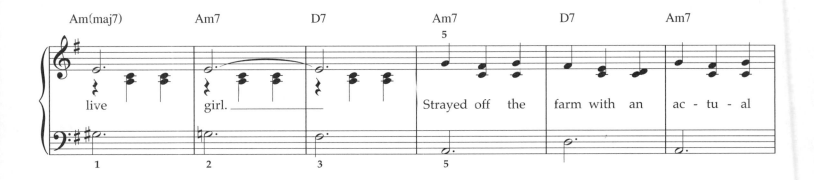

live girl. Strayed off the farm with an ac-tu-al

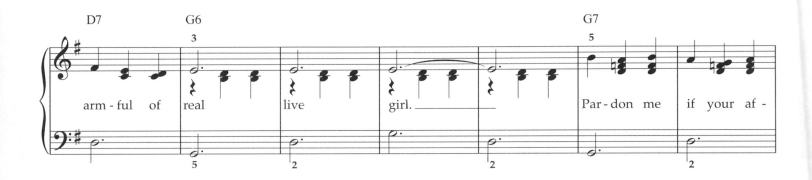

arm-ful of real live girl. Par-don me if your af-

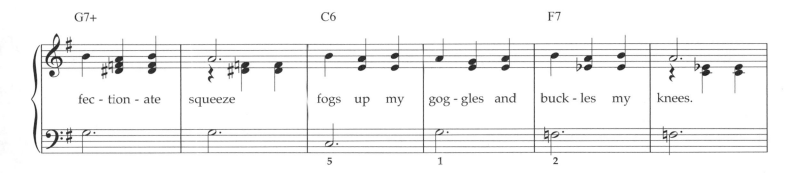

fec-tion-ate squeeze fogs up my gog-gles and buck-les my knees.

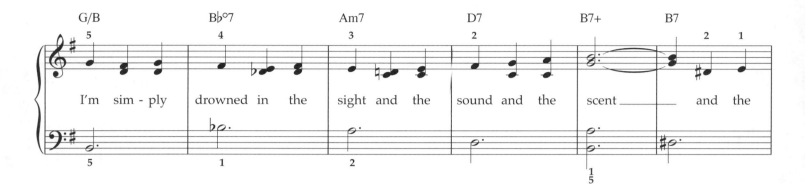

I'm sim-ply drowned in the sight and the sound and the scent_____ and the

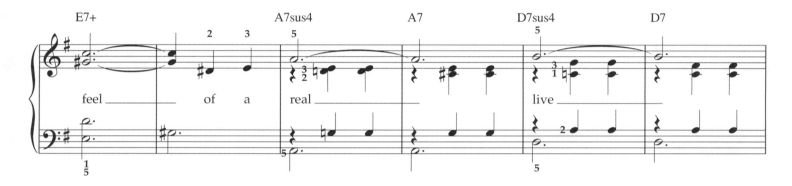

feel_____ of a real_____ live_____

girl._____ I've seen pho-to-graphs and fac-

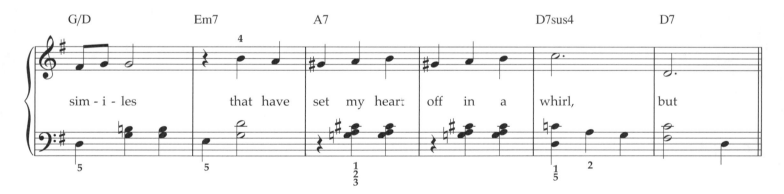

sim-i-les that have set my heart off in a whirl, but

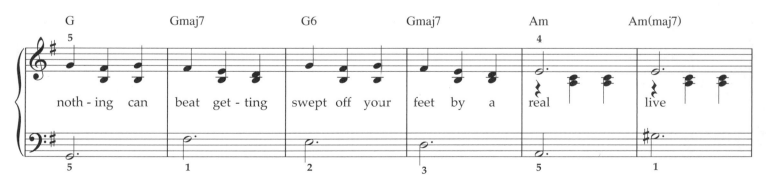

noth-ing can beat get-ting swept off your feet by a real_____ live

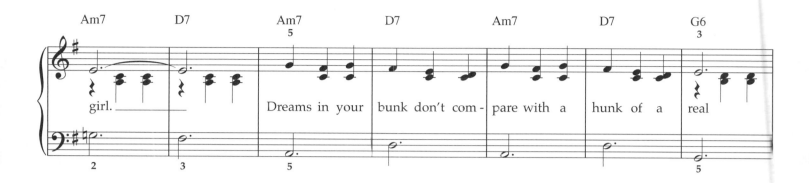

girl. Dreams in your bunk don't com-pare with a hunk of a real

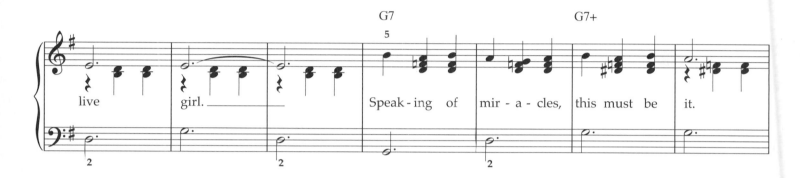

live girl. Speak-ing of mir-a-cles, this must be it.

Just when I start-ed to learn how to knit. I'm all in stitch-es from

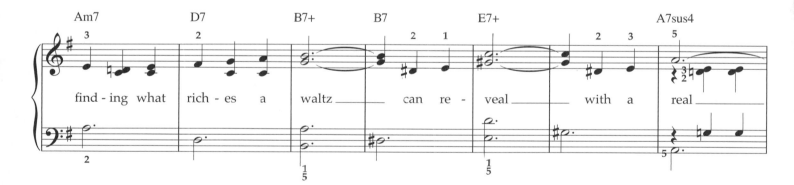

find-ing what rich-es a waltz can re-veal with a real

live girl. _mf_

The Phantom Of The Opera

from *THE PHANTOM OF THE OPERA*

Music by Andrew Lloyd Webber
Lyrics by Charles Hart
Additional Lyrics by Richard Stilgoe and Mike Batt

Moderately fast

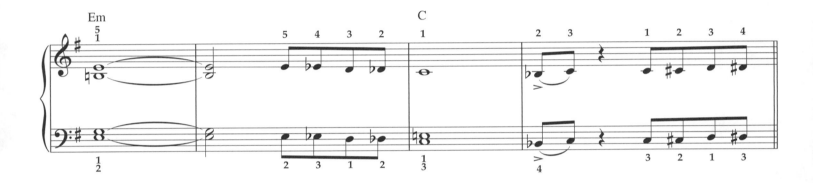

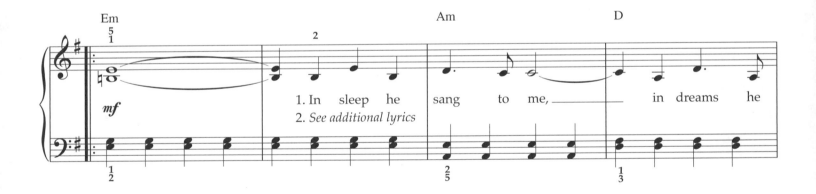

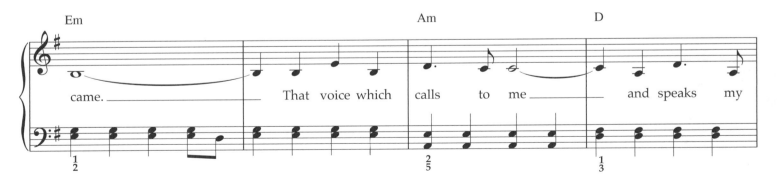

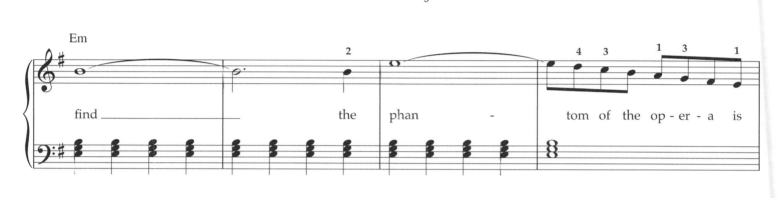

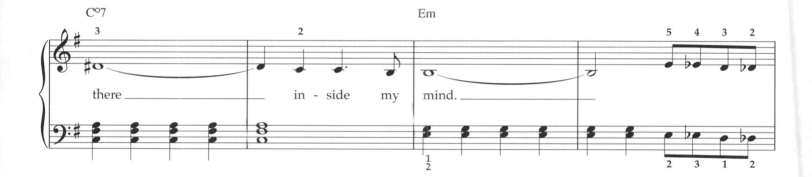

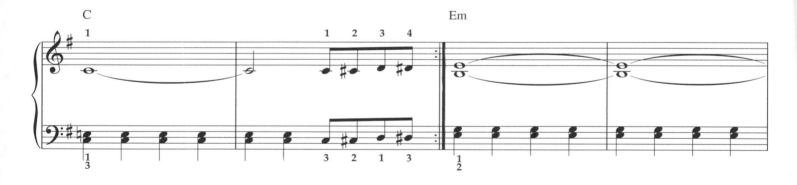

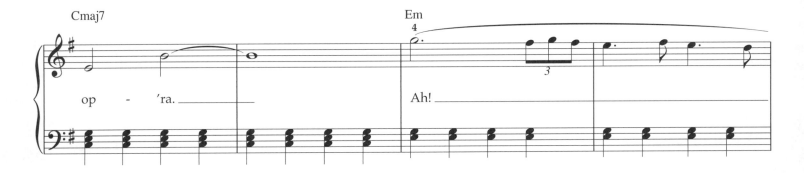

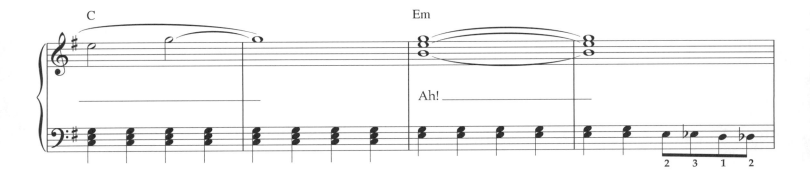

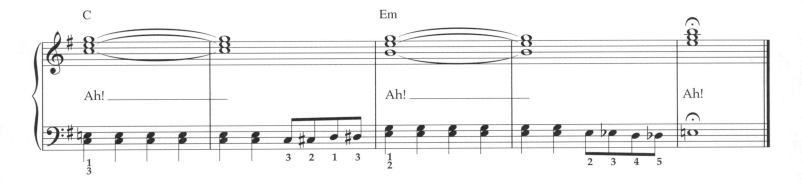

Additional lyrics

2. Sing once again with me our strange duet;
   My power over you grows stronger yet.
   And though you turn from me to glance behind,
   The phantom of the opera is there inside your mind.

3. Those who have seen your face draw back in fear.
   I am the mask you wear, it's me they hear.
   My spirit and my voice in one combined:
   The phantom of the opera is there inside your mind.

4. In all your fantasies, you always knew
   That men and mystery were both in you.
   And in this labyrinth where night is blind,
   The phantom of the opera is there inside your mind.

Some Enchanted Evening

from *SOUTH PACIFIC*

Lyrics by Oscar Hammerstein II
Music by Richard Rodgers

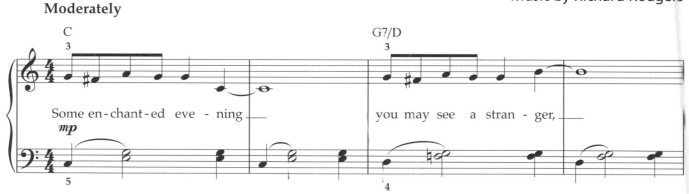

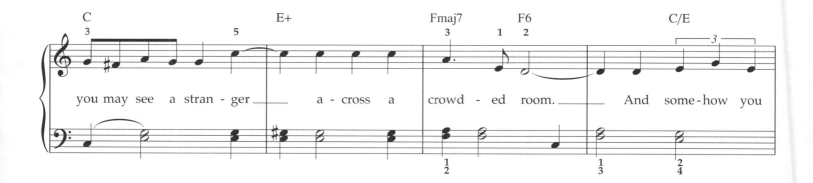

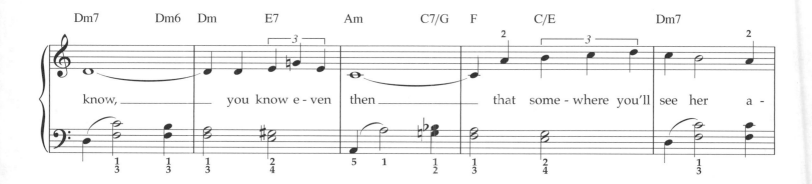

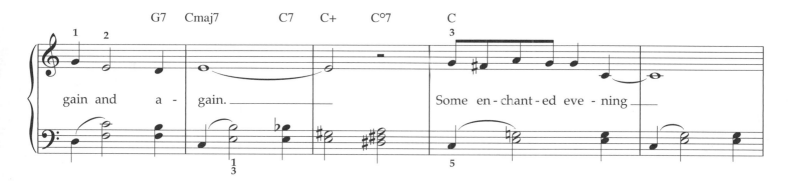

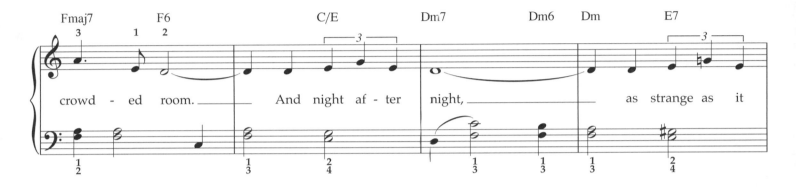

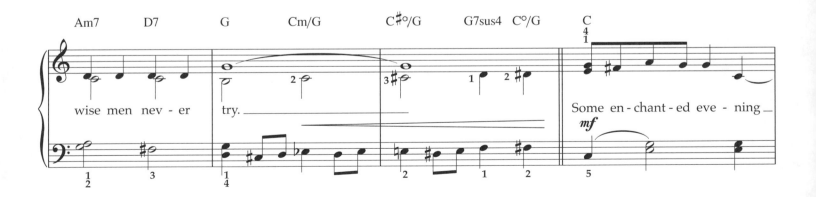

when you find your true love, ___ when you hear her call you ___

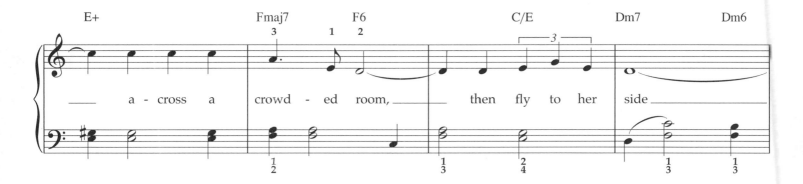

___ a - cross a crowd - ed room, ___ then fly to her side ___

___ and make her your own. ___ Or all through your life you may dream all a -

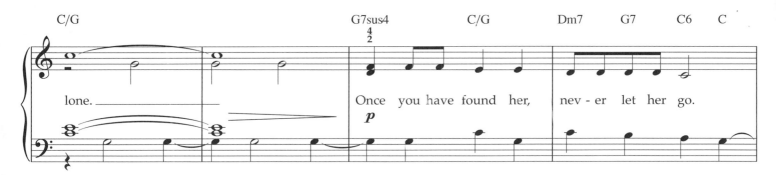

lone. ___ Once you have found her, nev - er let her go.

Once you have found her, nev - er let her go. ___

That Face
from *THE PRODUCERS*

Music and Lyrics by Mel Brooks

Moderately fast, in 2

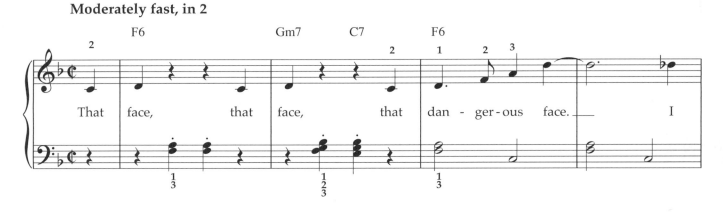

That face, that face, that dan-ger-ous face.____ I

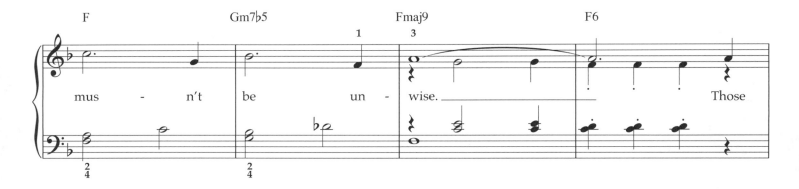

mus - n't be un - wise.____ Those

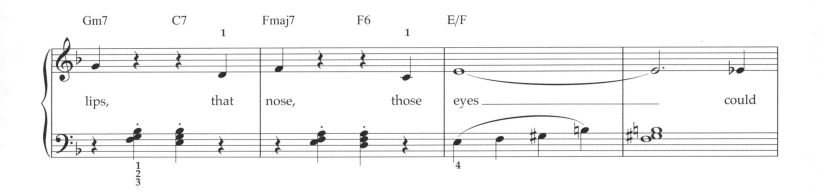

lips, that nose, those eyes _____ could

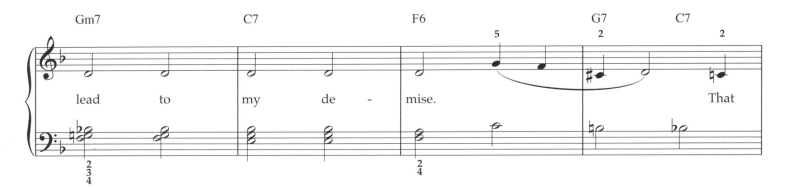

lead to my de - mise. That

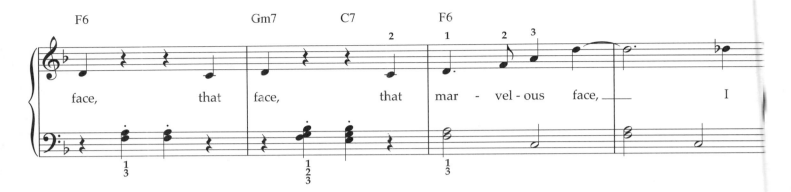

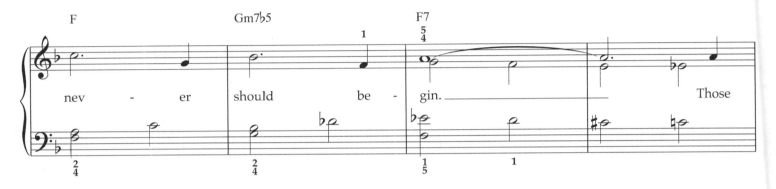

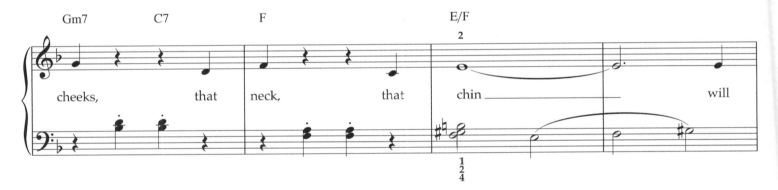

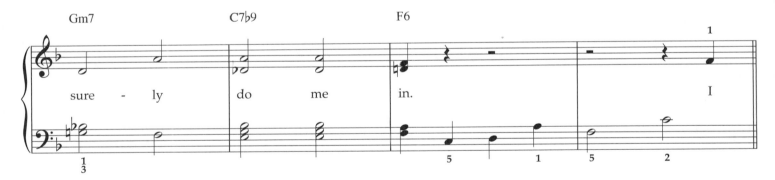

Slower

I don't duck, I'm out of luck. She'd kill me with her smile. That

A Tempo

face, that face, that fab - u - lous face, it's

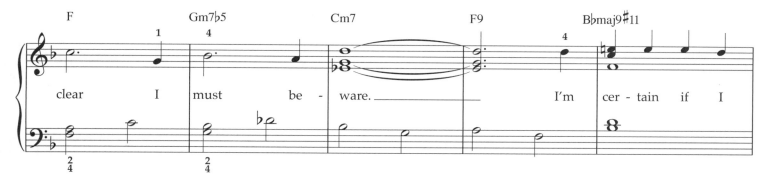

clear I must be - ware. I'm cer - tain if I

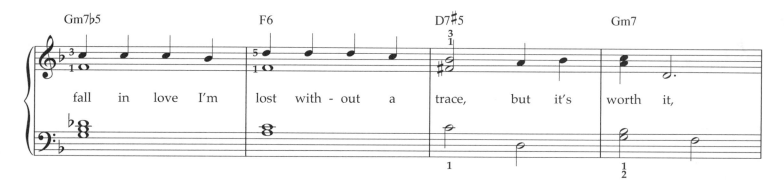

fall in love I'm lost with - out a trace, but it's worth it,

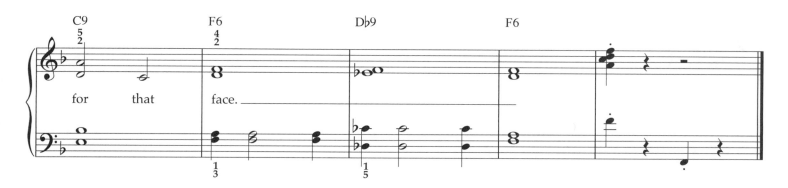

for that face.

Tell Me On A Sunday
from *SONG & DANCE*

Music by Andrew Lloyd Webber
Lyrics by Don Black

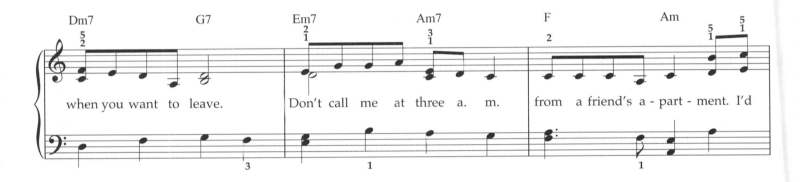

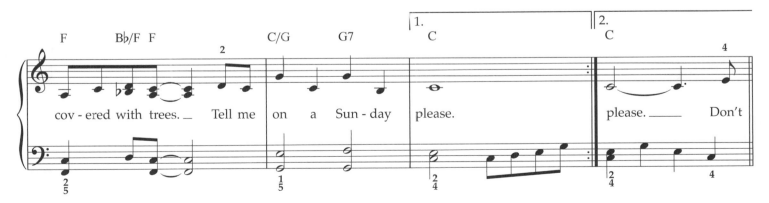

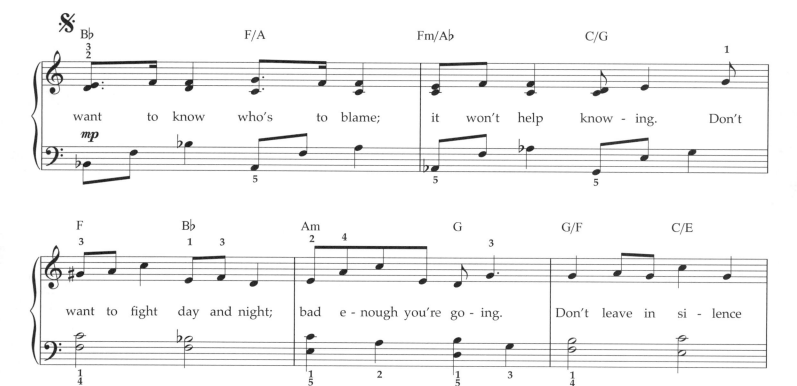

want to know who's to blame; it won't help know - ing. Don't

want to fight day and night; bad e - nough you're go - ing. Don't leave in si - lence

with no word at all. Don't get drunk and slam the door; that's no way to end this. I

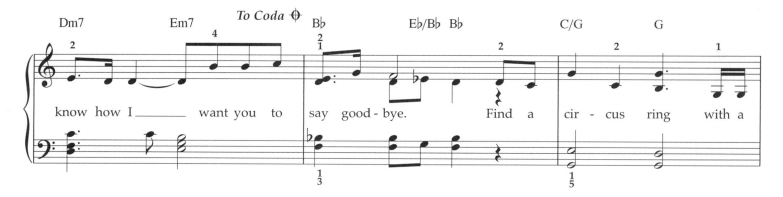

know how I _____ want you to say good - bye. Find a cir - cus ring with a

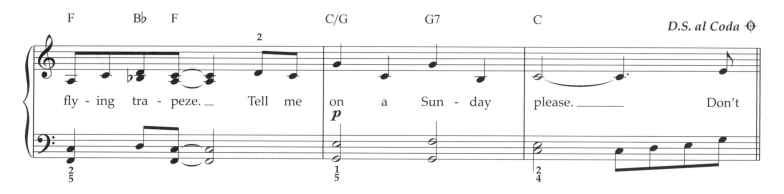

fly - ing tra - peze. ___ Tell me on a Sun - day please. _____ Don't

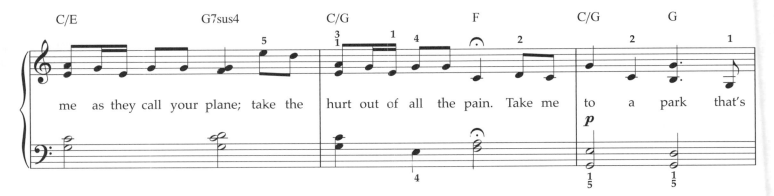

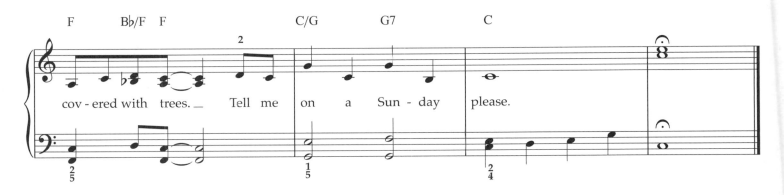

Additional lyrics

2. Let me down easy, no big song and dance.
No long faces, no long looks,
No deep conversation.
I know the way we should spend that day:
Take me to a zoo that's got chimpanzees.
Tell me on a Sunday please.

A Wonderful Guy

from *SOUTH PACIFIC*

Lyrics by Oscar Hammerstein II
Music by Richard Rodgers

Moderately bright waltz

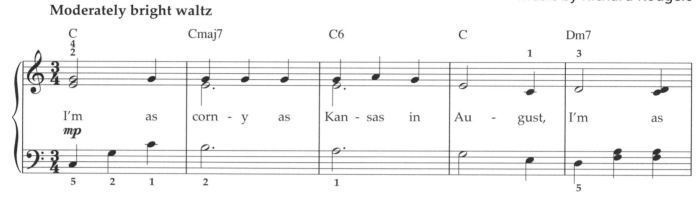

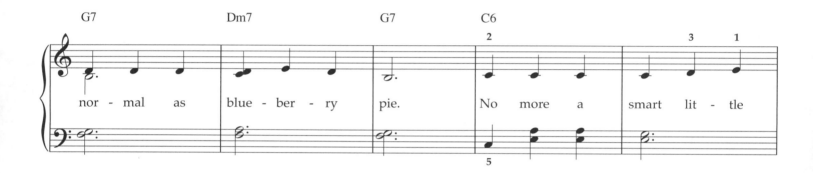

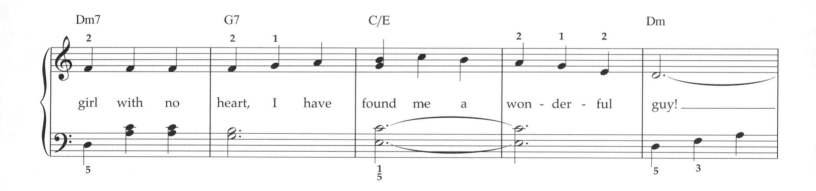

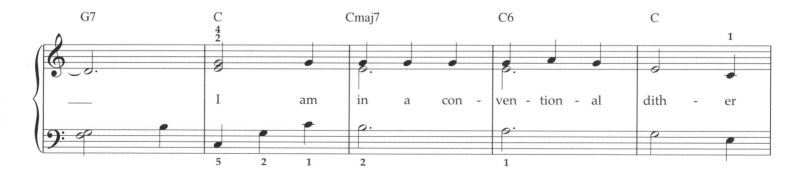

with a con - ven - tion - al star in my eye. And you will

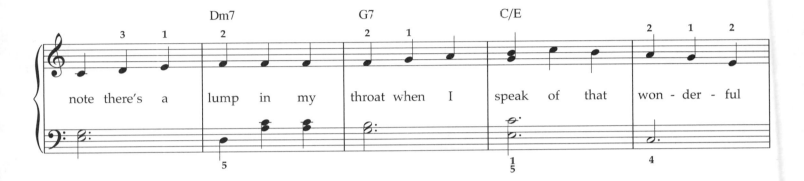

note there's a lump in my throat when I speak of that won - der - ful

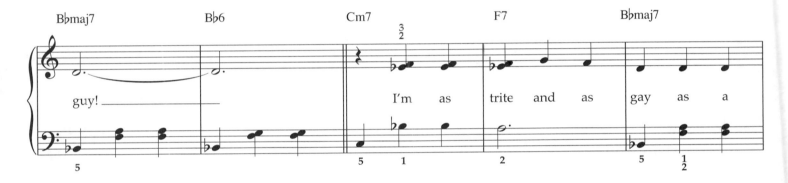

guy! _____ I'm as trite and as gay as a

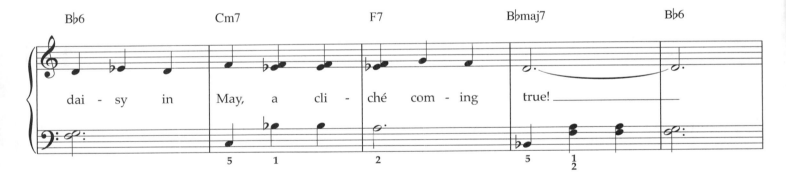

dai - sy in May, a cli - ché com - ing true! _____

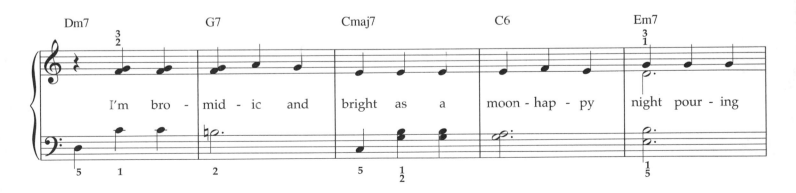

I'm bro - mid - ic and bright as a moon - hap - py night pour - ing

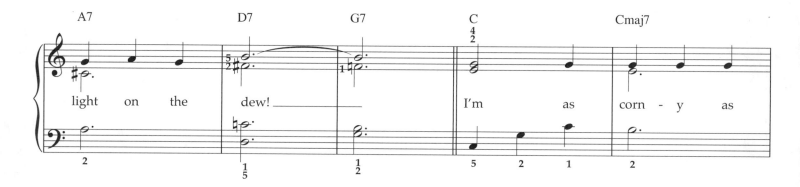

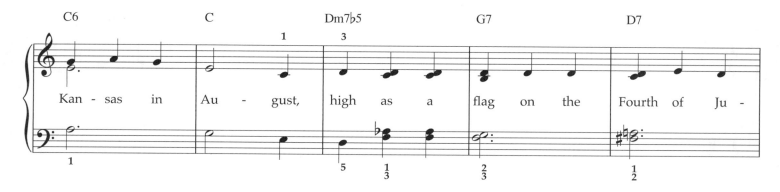

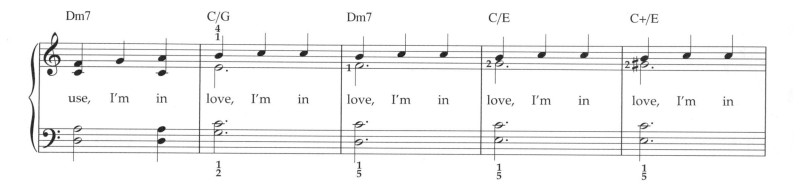

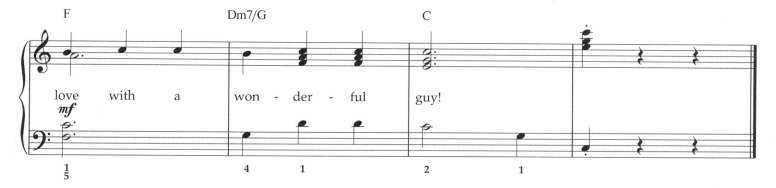